WHO IS JESUS?

GAËLLE TERTRAIS • ADELINE AVRIL

WHO IS JESUS?

HIS LIFE • HIS LAND • HIS TIME

MAGNIFICAT • Ignatius

CONTENTS

I THE PEOPLE OF ISRAEL

One truly extraordinary event has occurred in
the history of mankind: the birth of Jesus.
But it didn't happen just anywhere or just whenever!
God had, so to speak, prepared the groundwork. First, he
chose a people, the Hebrews, with whom he made a covenant.
Then he gave them a land, Israel. For almost 2,000 years, God
patiently prepared this people to know him and love him.

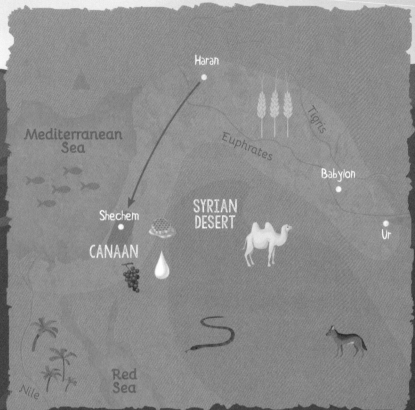

⭐ **Abraham's journey to the land of Canaan**

Abraham

The Hebrew nation, from which Jesus descended, is an ancient people with a turbulent history. It all began with Abraham, about 2,000 years before Jesus was born.

Abraham was from the city of Ur, in Mesopotamia (in the south of present-day Iraq).

One day, in Haran, God spoke to Abraham and made a **covenant** with him. He promised him a land and numerous descendants who would be a blessing to all the peoples of the world. Abraham believed God's word and set out with his family and his flocks. After a journey of almost 375 miles, he arrived in **Canaan**, the land promised by God.

The patriarchs

Abraham's descendants—first Isaac, then Jacob (whom God renamed Israel) and his twelve sons—eventually became a great nation: the people of Israel. Abraham, Isaac, and Jacob were the founding fathers of this people. That's why they are called the **patriarchs**. Jacob's twelve sons and their descendants were the origin of the **twelve tribes of Israel**.

★ The family tree of the patriarchs

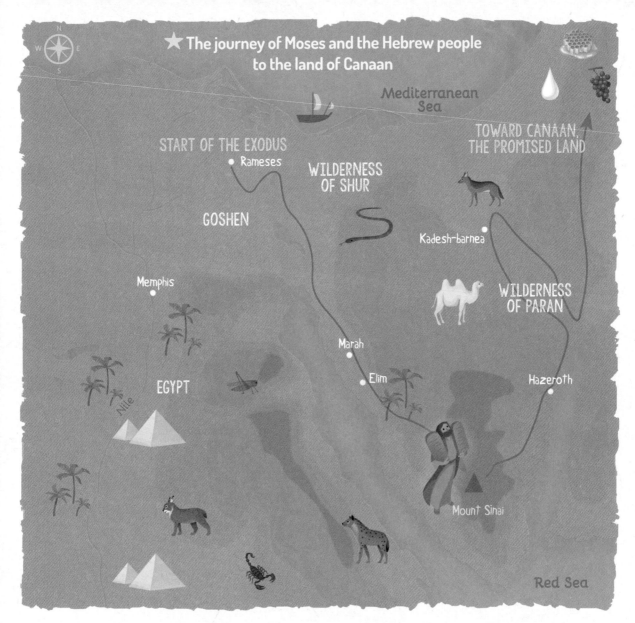

Mediterranean Sea

START OF THE EXODUS

TOWARD CANAAN, THE PROMISED LAND

Rameses

WILDERNESS OF SHUR

GOSHEN

Kadesh-barnea

Memphis

WILDERNESS OF PARAN

Marah

EGYPT

Elim

Hazeroth

Nile

Mount Sinai

Red Sea

Moses and the giving of the Law

Around the year 1800 B.C., when a famine struck the land of Canaan, Jacob's sons left to settle in Egypt. Four hundred years later, their then numerous descendants had been reduced to slavery by the Egyptians. But God did not forget his covenant with his people. He chose Moses to free the Hebrews from the Egyptians and to lead them back to their land of Canaan.

It took the Hebrews forty years to get back to the Promised Land. During this long march across the desert—a time called the **Exodus**—the people doubted and rebelled, but then returned to God.

God gave them the Law, the **Ten Commandments** engraved on stone tablets, to teach people how to live together in peace by respecting him and each other. These tablets of the Law were kept in a precious chest: the **ark of the covenant**. It was there that God dwelled among his people.

The judges and the kings

After forty years in the desert, the Hebrews still had to reclaim the land of Canaan. **Jericho** was the first city they conquered. The Bible tells the story: for seven days, the Hebrews marched around the city walls carrying the ark of the covenant, with seven priests at the lead, playing trumpets. On the seventh day, the city walls came tumbling down! The twelve tribes of Israel then divided the land of Canaan between them.

At that time, the people of Israel followed the leadership of **judges**. Among them were Gideon and Samson. Occasionally, they were women, such as Deborah. But soon the people asked to have a king to be like all the other nations. **Saul** became the first king of Israel. His reign was followed by that of the great King **David**, which lasted nearly forty years. His son **Solomon**, famed for his wisdom, is the one who built the Temple in Jerusalem to house the ark of the covenant.

In the 8th century before Jesus Christ, the prophet Isaiah foretold the coming of a child who would be the Son of God. Here's one of his prophecies: *Behold, a virgin shall conceive and bear a son, and shall call his name Immanuel* [which means "God-with-us"].

(Isaiah 7:14)

★ The anointing of the king

The kings of Israel were consecrated by pouring olive oil on their head. It was a sacred anointing meant to demonstrate to all that the proper authority of the king came from God.

Did you know?

The word "prophet" comes from a Greek word meaning "the one who announces." A prophet is a messenger of God.

The prophets

In 930 B.C., the people of Israel divided into two kingdoms: the **kingdom of Israel**, in the north, and the **kingdom of Judah**, in the south, with **Jerusalem** as its capital. But the two kingdoms were unfaithful to God and turned to pagan gods like Baal.

God sent his people **prophets**, his messengers, to encourage them to return to him. Among these were Samuel, Elijah, Elisha, Jonah, Amos, Hosea, Isaiah, Micah,

Zephaniah, Jeremiah, Ezekiel, Daniel, Zechariah, and Malachi. They never stopped reminding the people of God's love for them, and prophesying the misfortunes that would befall them if they didn't abandon their wicked ways. They also announced the coming of the Savior.

Then for 400 years there were no more prophets, until the birth of John the Baptist, the cousin of Jesus.

The Babylonian exile

Catastrophe struck Israel when King **Nebuchadnezzar** attacked Jerusalem in 586 B.C. He demolished the Temple and took part of the population as captives to **Babylon**. Their exile lasted seventy years.

Far from their homeland, the children of Israel tried to retain their Jewish culture and identity. They turned away from the pagan gods of their conquerors to worship the one true God and to keep the Law he revealed to Moses. Deprived of the Temple, where they had offered prayers and sacrifices, the Hebrews built **synagogues**, where they could gather to pray and to read the Scriptures. The Jewish religion as it is known today took shape during the exile.

But the people of Israel still dreamed of returning to their own country (as Psalm 137 sings about). And it finally happened in 538 B.C., when Persian Emperor **Cyrus** captured Babylon and freed the Israelites. At last, they returned to their homeland, and immediately rebuilt the Temple in Jerusalem.

Not everyone returned to Israel. Some stayed in Babylon; others settled in Morocco, or even in India. Many Jews also left for Egypt. This scattering of the Jewish people is known as the **diaspora**.

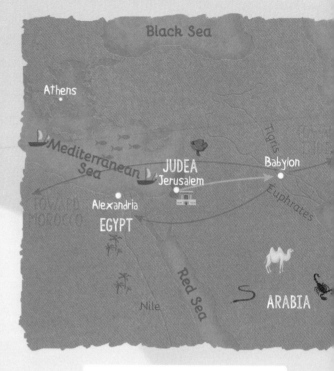

★ The scattering of the Jewish people throughout the world after the Babylonian exile

Black Sea

Athens

Mediterranean Sea

JUDEA
Jerusalem

Alexandria

EGYPT

TOWARD MOROCCO

Nile

Red Sea

Tigris

Babylon

Euphrates

ARABIA

⟶ The deportation to Babylon
⟵ The disapora

By the waters of Babylon,
there we sat down and wept,
when we remembered Zion.
On the willows there
we hung up our lyres.

(Psalm 137:1-2)

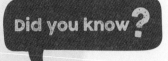

Did you know?

Zion is another name for Jerusalem,
after the name of the mountain
on which the city was built.

Did you know?

After the Babylonian exile, the Israelites who repopulated
Israel were mainly descendants of the tribe of Judah. It was
then that they became known as "Jews," from the name of
Judah, who also gave his name to the region of Judea.

★ The empire of Alexander the Great, from Macedon to India

BRITANNIA

GERMANIA

GAUL

ITALIA

Rome ●

Black Sea

IBERIA

MACEDON

ASIA MINOR

ARMENIA

NUMIDIA

Mediterranean Sea

Babylon ●

Alexandria ●

Jerusalem

CYRENAICA

EGYPT

Red Sea

■ The conquests of Alexander the Great
■ Roman empire in the 4th century B.C.

★ Coin stamped with the portrait of Antiochus IV Epiphanes

Did you know?

Maccabeus means "hammer." This was the nickname given to Judas, the son of Mattathias, who became the leader of the resistance against the tyrannical rule of Antiochus.

INDIA

Indian Ocean

Under foreign rule

Even back in their own country, the people of Israel had to fight to keep their independence. In 336 B.C., **Alexander the Great** came to power in Greece (then called Macedon). He made conquest after conquest, all the way to India. After he captured the land of Israel, some Jews gave in to the attractions of Greek culture.

In 169 B.C., the king of Syria, **Antiochus IV Epiphanes**, invaded Israel and sacked the Temple. He forced the people to adopt Greek customs and religion. Those who refused were put to death. One group of faithful Jews, led by the priest Mattathias, were determined to resist. This was the **revolt of the Maccabees**. Their rebellion was victorious, and the family of the Maccabees then led Judea.

The misfortunes of the people of Israel weren't over yet. Intrigues and wars shook the country until the Romans invaded in 63 B.C.. Under Roman rule, the people of Israel hoped more than ever for the coming of the Messiah, the Savior promised by God and foretold by the prophets, who would free them from foreign occupation.

2 THE ROMAN EMPIRE

Located at the crossroads between Europe, Asia, and Africa, Israel was often invaded. In the time of Jesus, it was occupied by the Romans.

Israel in the time of Jesus

The frontiers of Israel had greatly changed over the course of the centuries. At the time of Jesus' birth, it was principally comprised of **Galilee** in the north, **Samaria** in the center, and **Judea** in the south. It was traversed by the Jordan River, which flows into the Dead Sea.

Galilee is a fertile region that borders the Sea of Galilee (also called Lake Tiberias or Lake Gennesaret). It has a mild climate: olive trees, grapevines, wheat, and fig trees all grow there in abundance. Jews and Gentiles (non-Jews) lived there together in harmony. Many **fishing villages** bordered its shores, including Bethsaida and Capernaum, which Jesus often visited. The countryside was studded with **farming villages**, such as Cana, where Jesus performed his first miracle, and Nazareth, where Jesus grew up. Tiberias was a **new town** built in honor of Emperor Tiberias. The port of Caesarea was built by King Herod in honor of Caesar.

WHO WERE THE PAGANS?

For the Jews in the time of Jesus, pagans were those who did not know the one God of Israel and worshiped other gods.

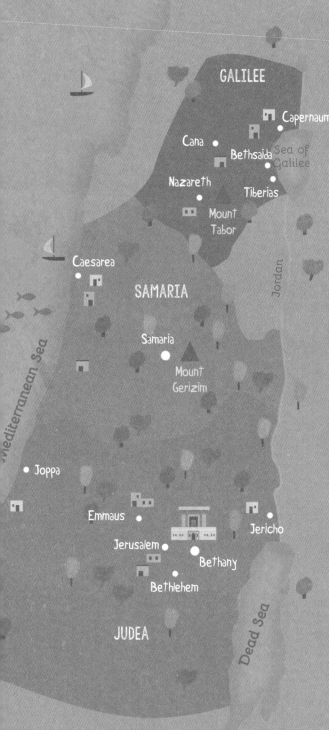

GALILEE

Capernaum

Cana

Bethsaida

Sea of Galilee

Nazareth

Tiberias

Mount Tabor

Caesarea

SAMARIA

Jordan

Samaria

Mount Gerizim

Mediterranean Sea

Joppa

Emmaus

Jericho

Jerusalem

Bethany

Bethlehem

JUDEA

Dead Sea

SINAI DESERT

At 1,400 feet below sea level, the shores of the Dead Sea are at the lowest altitude on earth.

Samaria takes its name from its capital, Samaria. Its population was not of Jewish origin, but they observed the Law of Moses. The people worshiped God not in Jerusalem but on **Mount Gerizim**. The Jews of Judea and Galilee considered the Samaritans ungodly, and hated them. They would avoid passing through Samaria.

Judea, with **Jerusalem** as its capital, is a dry, mountainous region. Its population was almost exclusively comprised of pious Jews. Jerusalem, with the Temple and Herod's palace, was the political and religious hub of the land. The main cities were Jericho, in the Jordan Valley, Emmaus, and Joppa (present-day Jaffa), on the Mediterranean coast.

In the mountains, six miles or so from Jerusalem, is the little village of **Bethlehem**, where Jesus was born.

★ The land of Israel in the time of Jesus

HEROD AND THE ROMANS

The Roman invasion

Shortly before the birth of Jesus, Judea was invaded by the Romans. General Pompey captured Jerusalem in 63 B.C. The Roman Empire was occupying the entire Mediterranean basin. Certain lands were annexed by the empire and became Roman provinces (like Syria), while others were occupied but kept their own governments (like Judea, at first).

And so the kingdom of Judea became a Roman dependency, where the Romans made their presence felt with military garrisons and heavy taxes.

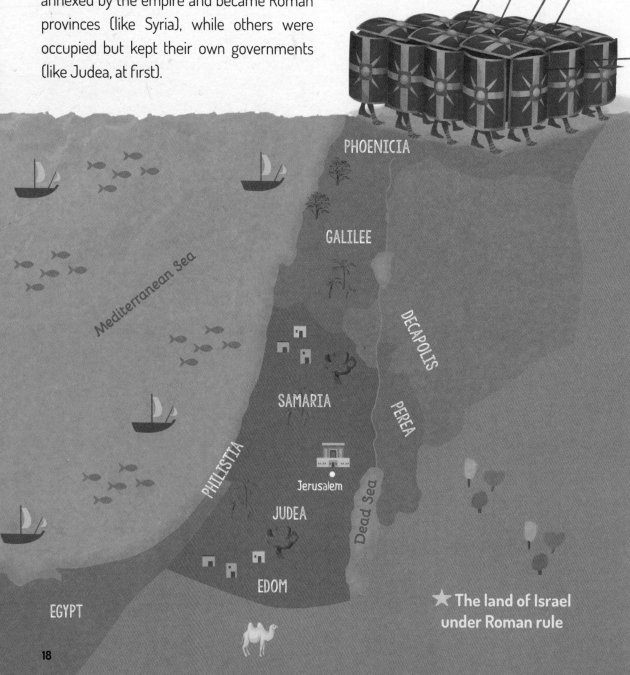

PHOENICIA

GALILEE

Mediterranean Sea

DECAPOLIS

SAMARIA

PEREA

PHILISTIA

Jerusalem

Dead Sea

JUDEA

EDOM

EGYPT

★ The land of Israel under Roman rule

Herod the Great

The Romans themselves appointed the king of Judea: **Herod the Great** (37 to 4 B.C.), the son of Antipas. He was not of Jewish origin; he came from Edom, and his mother was Arabian. It was during his reign that Jesus was born. A prophecy had foretold that the Messiah would be born during the reign of a king who was not of Jewish origin.

The Jews did not like Herod. He even had to lay siege to Jerusalem to impose his rule. He was a cruel king, and so jealous of his power that he had his first wife and several of his sons murdered!

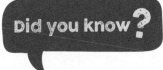

The Romans called all of Israel "Judea," from the name of the tribe of Judah. In reality, this province included Judea, Samaria, and Edom.

He was also a great builder of palaces (Jericho, Masada), of temples dedicated to Roman gods, and of cities (Caesarea Maritima). But his greatest work was the restoration of the **Jerusalem Temple**, which he enlarged to gain popularity with the Jews. Upon his death, his kingdom was divided among his three sons. Judea and Samaria went to Archelaus, Galilee to Herod Antipas, and the small territories in the north to Philip.

But in A.D. 6, Archelaus was deposed, and Judea and Samaria became Roman provinces run by a Roman procurator, a precursor of Pontius Pilate. From then on, the Romans were the true masters of the land.

★ Herod the Great

★ Joseph and Mary

3 THE BIRTH AND CHILDHOOD OF JESUS

The birth of Jesus remains the most important event in all of history. We count years before (B.C.) and after (A.D.) the birth of Christ.

Who is Jesus?

The Evangelists Matthew and Luke, who tell the story of the birth of Jesus, present him as the son of Mary, a young woman from Nazareth, and foster son of Joseph, a carpenter from the same village. Through his family tree, Matthew shows that Jesus was a descendant of King David through Joseph, and traces his origins all the way back to Abraham.

The Annunciation

While Mary was engaged to Joseph, the **angel Gabriel** appeared to her at home in Nazareth. He foretold that she would become the mother of a child who would be the Son of God. Mary trustingly said "Yes" to the angel. According to Luke, Mary was then overshadowed by the Holy Spirit, and from that moment, Mary was pregnant with the Son of God.

In a dream, **Joseph** also saw the angel Gabriel, who said that Mary's child was from God. He told Joseph that he should not fear to take Mary as his wife and to raise the child as his own. And so Joseph became Jesus' foster father.

MARY, THE GIRL FROM NAZARETH

Mary was a young woman from Nazareth. Her parents were Anne and Joachim. According to Christian tradition, they had been unable to have children. But, after much prayer, they had Mary. When she was about fourteen or fifteen, she was engaged to Joseph the carpenter. In that time, girls often became engaged as young as twelve. Joseph would have been a little bit older than she was.

THE ANGEL GABRIEL

Angels are found throughout the Bible. Some had more important missions than others. Only three are named: the archangels Gabriel, Michael, and Raphael. Their names reveal their missions. Gabriel means "God is my strength"; Michael, "Who is like God?"; and Raphael, "God heals."

The Visitation

The angel Gabriel also informed Mary that her elderly cousin **Elizabeth** was expecting a baby, too. In Jewish society, being unable to bear a child was considered shameful. Mary left right away to visit her cousin, to help her. Elizabeth greeted her with the cry, *Blessed are you among women, and blessed is the fruit of your womb* (Luke 1:42). Elizabeth understood that Mary was the mother of the Savior. The child Elizabeth was carrying (the future John the Baptist) also recognized the **Messiah**, and he leaped for joy in his mother's womb!

★ The angel Gabriel

Did you know?

The life of Jesus is told in the four Gospels of Matthew, Mark, Luke, and John. Matthew and John were Apostles of Jesus; Mark was a friend of Peter the Apostle; and Luke was a doctor and a traveling companion of the Apostle Paul.

THE FEAST DAYS OF MARY

Catholics celebrate the Immaculate Conception of Mary on December 8, her birth on September 8, and her Assumption on August 15. We remember the Annunciation on March 25 and the Visitation on May 31. We honor her as Mother of God on January 1 and as Our Lady of Guadalupe on December 12. And she has many other feast days, 17 in total.

THE BIRTH OF JESUS

★ The basilica in Bethlehem

The census

Just before Jesus was born, Roman Emperor Augustus decided to count the entire population of his immense empire, of which Judea was a part. For this census, everyone was required to go to his village of origin to be registered. As a **descendant of David**, Joseph had to go with his wife to **Bethlehem**, the hometown of King David.

Because of this census, many people were on the move. In Bethlehem, there was no more room for Joseph and Mary in the inn, the place where visitors passing through could spend the night. In any case, it would not have been a private enough place to give birth to a baby.

Mary and Joseph found a quiet shelter in an unusual place for a birth: a stable. Saint Luke even tells us that baby Jesus was laid in a **manger**. A tradition dating back to the 2nd century identified this stable as a cave, or grotto, in Bethlehem. As in that mountainous region, natural caves were often used as stables, it's very probable that Jesus was born in a grotto. In the 4th century, Emperor Constantine the Great had a basilica built over a Bethlehem grotto traditionally thought to be the birthplace of Jesus. It is one of the oldest churches in the world.

Did you know?

The French word "crèche" initially meant the manger where hay was put for the animals. By extension, it referred to the whole stable and, in time, the one where Jesus was born.

What's in a name?

In Hebrew, **Bethlehem** means "house of bread."

Christmas in the spring?

On the night of the birth of Jesus, **shepherds** were watching over their flocks in the nearby fields. Suddenly, angels appeared and announced the birth of Jesus to them. The shepherds ran to Bethlehem and found the baby Jesus in the manger.

Dionysius Exiguus set the date of Christmas as December 25 to replace the Roman feast of the "birthday of the unconquered sun," which in Latin is *Dies natalis solis invicti* (the word "nativity" is related to the word *natalis*). This feast was on the **winter solstice**. Celebrating Christmas then says that Jesus is like the sun who conquers the night. But the presence of the shepherds indicates that Jesus was not born in the middle of winter, for sheep were pastured in the fields between the months of March and November. The rest of the year, it's too cold for them to spend the night outside!

What's more, Bethlehem is near Jerusalem. In March and April, many flocks were led to the Temple to provide sacrificial animals for the feast of **Passover** (to learn more about Passover, see page 85). So Jesus might have been born in March or April.

Surrounding a birth

The birth of a child was always a cause for celebration for the Jews, especially when the baby was a boy. A midwife would be present to help the mother give birth. At that time, Jewish women breastfed their child for two or three years.

Little Jewish boys are circumcised eight days after birth. **Circumcision** is the removal of the baby boy's foreskin, a custom that goes all the way back to Abraham. God asked him to do this to himself and to his son Isaac. This custom had already existed among other peoples, including the Egyptians, for example. It was at first practiced for reasons of hygiene. For the Jews it became a religious rite and a mark of thanksgiving. Jesus was circumcised according to his people's tradition.

At the time of circumcision, the father gives his son a name. It is generally chosen from among the names of other family members. In the case of Jesus, it was the angel Gabriel who told Mary the name of her future child: **Jesus**, which means **"God saves."**

Candlemas is an old name for the feast of the Presentation of Jesus in the Temple. Candles are blessed on this day for it celebrates when Jesus was revealed as the "light to the nations" to the elderly Simeon when he saw him in the Jerusalem Temple.

The Presentation in the Temple

Forty days after his birth, Jesus' parents took him to the Temple to be consecrated to God, as prescribed in the Law of Moses for every firstborn. According to tradition, parents symbolically "redeemed" their child by offering an animal sacrifice.

The Presentation in the Temple also corresponds to Mary's purification, which all women did forty days after giving birth. For this they had to offer a lamb or, if they were poor, a pair of turtledoves or pigeons.

An astonishing thing happened during Jesus' Presentation in the Temple. An old man named **Simeon** approached Joseph and Mary. God had told him that he would not die until he had seen the Messiah. That day, inspired by the Holy Spirit, he went to the Temple and saw Jesus. Taking him in his arms, he declared that he could now die in peace, for he had seen the Messiah awaited by Israel. The **Canticle of Simeon** is sung by Catholic priests, monks, and nuns every evening before retiring to bed.

⭐ The journey of the Magi

Magi who weren't kings

The Gospel of Matthew speaks of Magi who came from the East. The Greek word used is *magoï*, which we translate as **"Magi."** It is a word used for wise men or, more precisely, astrologers, who were many in Babylon and Persia. No doubt that was where the Magi came from.

However, there is no reason to believe that they were kings. Christian tradition gave them this title as an allusion to three Old Testament prophecies which said that kings would bow down before the Son of God. *May the kings of Tarshish and of the isles render him tribute, may the kings of Sheba and Seba bring gifts*, says one of them (Psalm 72:10).

A not-so-mysterious star

The star observed by the Magi moved through the sky. The word the Bible uses for this star is "comet." Chinese texts mention the appearance of a comet with a tail from March to April in 5 B.C. This comet may be the one seen by the Magi. As it orbited around the sun, it would disappear at times, exactly like the Magi's star, which disappeared from view during the journey from Jerusalem to Bethlehem.

Gold, frankincense, and myrrh

The three gifts mentioned by Matthew suggest there were three Magi. However, their number is not specified. They were gifts of great value and had highly symbolic meaning.

Gold is a royal gift. In offering it to Jesus, the Magi recognized him as the king of Israel.

Frankincense was used in the ceremonies of numerous religions as a divine offering. So the Magi recognized Jesus as God.

Myrrh was used to embalm the dead according to Jewish custom of the time. The Magi recognized Jesus as a man who, one day, would die.

Did you know?

The Magi must have visited the Holy Family when Jesus was about two years old. At that time, they were no longer living in a stable but probably in a little house in the village.

THE MOVE TO NAZARETH AND JESUS' CHILDHOOD

The massacre of the innocents and the flight into Egypt

A tragic event, recognized by historians, cast a shadow over the childhood of Jesus. On seeing the star that heralded the birth of the king of the Jews, the Magi went first to Jerusalem, to the palace of King Herod. In fear for his throne, Herod gave a horrible order: to kill all the Hebrew boys under the age of two (the Magi hadn't told him the precise age of the child) in the region of Bethlehem.

Warned in a dream by an angel, Joseph fled to Egypt with Mary and the child. This is how it came to be that Jesus spent his first years in a foreign country, the same one in which the Hebrews had been enslaved before being freed by Moses.

The move to Nazareth

After the death of Herod, an angel informed Joseph that it was safe to return to his country. The family left Egypt and settled in **Nazareth**, in Galilee. They didn't return to Bethlehem because Judea was in much turmoil under the rule of Herod's son Archelaus. Galilee, on the other hand, was peaceful: no Roman garrison was stationed in the village of Nazareth. Perhaps Jesus got to know his grandparents there, since that was where Mary and Joseph had grown up.

At that time, Nazareth was a little village of 200 inhabitants, nestled in a valley at the foot of a steep hill. Its water was supplied by a fountain outside the village, where Mary must have gone to draw water twice a day. The villagers grew wheat, barley or millet, grapevines, and olive trees. They raised flocks of sheep and goats.

The houses of the period were simple square boxes with whitewashed earthen walls. There was only one room, and the only light came through the door and sometimes a window. Their flat roofs were used as a terrace, reached by an outside stairway. People would sleep there in the summer when it was very hot.

JOSEPH THE CARPENTER

Joseph, the foster father of Jesus, was a carpenter. He taught his son his trade, as was the custom. In those days, the carpenter made tools and furniture, and the timber framework for houses, too. He had to be a bit of a stonemason as well as an architect. It was a respected trade. A carpenter was considered a learned man.

Did you know ?

Children played with dolls, carved wooden animals, and dice.

The education of children

Mary cooked the meals, did the housework, fetched water at the fountain, baked bread, spun and wove wool, and saw to Jesus' education. She no doubt taught Jesus **Holy Scripture**. Indeed, as soon as a child was able to talk, his mother would teach him to learn a few **verses of the Law** by heart.

Children didn't go to school but, from ages five to twelve or thirteen, they went to the synagogue on the sabbath day (see page 31) to learn to read verses of the Law that they memorized. Jesus also learned to write, at least a few letters. Children learned to trace letters on bits of pottery using chalk or coal. But formal writing was reserved to the scribes.

29

4 LIVING THE LAW OF MOSES

The Gospels tell us little about Jesus' childhood. Growing up in a Jewish family, his daily life would have been marked by the traditions inherited from the Law of Moses. The whole life of a Jew was, in fact, regulated by the Law.

Purifications, fasting, almsgiving

For Mary and Joseph, as for all Jewish families, every activity of the day was accompanied by a **prayer**. The father of the family would bless their meals, especially the bread and the wine. The light, too, was blessed, as were fire and water. Special prayers were said on every important occasion: a birth, a wedding, a funeral, a circumcision, the weaning of a baby.

Many **purification** rituals were prescribed by the Law. These most often entailed the washing of hands up to the wrist, for example, before a meal or upon returning from the market. In serious cases (such as touching a leper or a dead body), it was necessary to bathe completely. Certain foods were considered pure; others, like pork, were impure and forbidden.

The Law also laid out days of **fasting** (going without food) and the duty of **almsgiving**. There were three ways to give alms: giving money to a community collection box; giving to the synagogue, which collected money to distribute to the poor; and leaving a corner of one's field or vineyard unharvested, for the very poor to harvest themselves.

The sabbath

An important rule is to observe the sabbath, which is **Saturday**. This is a day of **celebration** and **joy**. On that day, thanks and praise are given to God for everything he has made. It is a day of **rest**, because God rested on the seventh day after he finished his creation. The sabbath begins at sunset on Friday evening. At that moment, the mother of the family lights the sabbath candles. She will have prepared the following day's meals in advance and cleaned the whole house.

A **list of thirty-nine rules** specifies what is forbidden to do on the sabbath. (You will find this list in chapter 9, page 75.)

THE LAW AND THE PROPHETS

For Jews in the time of Jesus, the holy texts were what we know as the **Old Testament**: the Law, the prophets, and the "writings." The Law, called the **Torah**, contains five books: Genesis, Exodus, Leviticus, Numbers, and Deuteronomy. It is sacred, containing the words God inspired Moses to write. The writings of the prophets, the history of the people of Israel, and the wisdom books were also considered the Word of God.

A RELIGIOUS SOCIETY

Jewish society was deeply religious. The Jewish day and calendar were marked by prayer.

Prayer

Jesus learned to pray within his family. Morning and evening, they recited the **Shema**, printed below, which begins with the words *Shema Yisrael*, meaning "Hear, O Israel." Three times a day, they also recited a long prayer of eighteen blessings called the **Shemoneh Esrei**, inspired by the psalms and the prophets.

Jews prayed standing up, facing toward Jerusalem, with the head covered in a white fringed shawl called a *talit*. During morning prayer, they wore little boxes called **phylacteries** (or *tephillin*), containing passages from the Torah written on a strip of parchment. The two phylacteries were attached by a thin strip of leather rolled seven times around the left arm (the side of the heart) for one, and placed on the forehead for the other.

Prayer was so important in the life of the Jews that, in order not to forget God's commandments, they wrote them on small pieces of parchment and kept them in a little box called a **mezuzah**, which they hung next to the doors of their houses.

Hear, O Israel: The LORD our God is one LORD; and you shall love the LORD your God with all your heart, and with all your soul, and with all your might. And these words which I command you this day shall be upon your heart; and you shall teach them diligently to your children, and shall talk of them when you sit in your house, and when you walk by the way, and when you lie down, and when you rise. And you shall bind them as a sign upon your hand, and they shall be as frontlets between your eyes. And you shall write them on the doorposts of your house and on your gates.

(Deuteronomy 6:4-9)

THE AGE OF RELIGIOUS MAJORITY

The Gospel of Luke tells of an episode in Jesus' childhood. When he was twelve, Jesus went on **pilgrimage to Jerusalem** with his parents for the feast of Passover. For Jesus, that pilgrimage was no doubt especially important. He was twelve years old, the age of religious majority for Jewish boys, after which they are required to respect the commandments of the Law as adults. If you would like to read this Gospel passage, you will find it in the Bible in Luke 2:41-51.

The synagogue

The synagogue is a **house of prayer**. People gathered there on the sabbath and for daily prayers. It was also a **meeting place** to study the Law, and a place of **celebration** for circumcisions, weddings, and funerals. But sacrifices were not practiced there, as in the Jerusalem Temple. It was led by wise men who knew the Law well, often scribes or Pharisees.

Men and women would go to the synagogue for morning, afternoon, and evening prayers. On the sabbath day, the morning service included hymns, psalms, and blessings, and readings of two texts from Holy Scripture (similar to our Liturgy of the Word). These readings were done in **Hebrew**, then translated into the local language. In Nazareth, Jesus listened to these texts in **Aramaic**, the language spoken in Galilee.

★ **A synagogue**

The synagogue was most often a simple rectangular room, sometimes embellished with four rows of columns. The scribes sat on a raised platform with a kind of pulpit and a **sacred cabinet** containing the holy books rolled up in linen cloth and placed in a case. In front of the cabinet was a curtain, reminiscent of the veil of the Temple. The room was furnished with benches. Mint leaves were scattered on the floor to perfume and purify the air. The front seats were reserved for the **doctors of the Law, Pharisees,** and important local personages. They sat facing the people. Men and women were separated, as in the Temple.

THE SCROLLS OF THE TORAH

The sacred texts are written on parchment attached to two wooden handles that can be unrolled as one reads. It is read from right to left with the aid of a pointer to help follow the lines without touching the parchment.

5 THE BAPTISM OF JESUS

Shortly before Jesus began his public life, an astonishing person appeared on the scene: John the Baptist. He was the last prophet.

John, a child chosen by God

John was a close relative of Jesus. Right from the start, his life was singled out for a particular destiny. Already when the expectant Mary visited her cousin Elizabeth, at the approach of Jesus, John leaped for joy in his mother's womb.

His parents, Elizabeth and Zechariah, hadn't been able to have children. Zechariah was a priest. While he was ministering in the Temple, the angel Gabriel appeared to him and foretold that he would have a son who would be called John. Zechariah couldn't believe it, and was struck speechless. And yet, despite her age, Elizabeth became pregnant. There are other examples of miraculous conceptions in the Bible: Isaac, the son of Abraham and Sarah; Samuel, the son of Hannah and Elkanah; and Samson, the son of Manoah. In each case, the child's fate was to have a decisive impact on the history of the people of Israel.

Upon the birth of John, Zechariah regained his speech, named his child, and foretold that he would be a great prophet who would prepare the coming of the Savior.

The **Canticle of Zechariah** is prayed by Catholic priests, monks, and nuns each morning.

HIS NAME IS JOHN

what's in a name?

In Hebrew, **John** means "God is gracious."

John, the last prophet

There had been no prophets since Malachi, in the 5th century B.C. But, acccording to one popular tradition, the prophet **Elijah** would return just before the coming of the Messiah. For many, John the Baptist was this new Elijah. He was **the last prophet**, the one who would form the link between the Old and the New Testaments.

In the Bible, the Old Testament tells the whole history of the Hebrew people up to the birth of Jesus, and the New Testament starts with the birth of John.

John the Baptist fulfilled the words of the prophet Isaiah: *The voice of one crying in the wilderness: Prepare the way of the Lord, make his paths straight.*

(Matthew 3:3)

The desert

John lived as a hermit in the Judean desert. In the history of the Jewish people, the desert is the place to which one withdraws to encounter God, as **Moses** and **Elijah** did, for example.

The Judean desert stretches from Jerusalem to the Dead Sea and the Jordan Valley. It is a rocky landscape of chalky hills, steep valleys, mountains, and cliffs. A few watercourses flow through the beds of the deep canyons, forming oases here and there.

The desert was uninhabited by man, but **animals** lived there. Some were harmless, like camels, ibexes, gazelles, marmots, and grasshoppers; others were more dangerous: hawks, scorpions, and snakes. It was also the kingdom of wild animals such as leopards, wolves, lynxes, hyenas, and jackals.

Hawk

Leopard

Wolf

Hyena

Jackal

Snake

Grasshopper

Scorpion

A LAND FLOWING WITH MILK AND HONEY

When God spoke to Moses from the burning bush, he promised his people a land flowing with milk and honey.

Milk was part of the basic diet of nomadic peoples who traveled with their flocks. It was a symbol of abundance and prosperity.

Honey symbolized sweetness and goodness. Much wild honey can be found in the rocks and the tree trunks of Israel. The Hebrews also developed beekeeping and exported honey to Tyre.

Locusts and wild honey

The Gospel of Matthew recounts that John the Baptist wore a tunic of camel's hair with a leather belt around his waist, and that he fed on **locusts** and **wild honey**. The land of Israel was overflowing with honey in the time of the Old Testament and was still so in the time of Jesus. Locusts were part of the daily diet in the East. They were roasted or cooked in salty water, or, after removing their legs and their heads, they were sun-dried and ground into a powder using a mortar. This powder produced a flour that gave bread a rather bitter taste. It was eaten with camel's milk and honey.

Lynx

Ibex

Camel

Marmot

Gazelle

The baptism of Jesus

John was baptizing people in the **Jordan River**, in a spot where there was deep water, for baptisms were done by immersion, by plunging the person into the water completely. The baptism John performed was a **baptism of conversion**: the baptized person publicly confessed his sins and promised to change his life.

One day, Jesus went to see John and asked to be baptized. Even though they were cousins, they had never met before! Yet John the Baptist recognized him right away and declared, *Behold, the Lamb of God, who takes away the sin of the world!*

Jesus didn't need to be baptized; he had no sin to confess, since he is God. But in asking John to baptize him, Jesus agreed to take upon himself all the sins of the world. That is the meaning of the words of John the Baptist.

At the moment Jesus rose up out of the water, a voice was heard coming from heaven: *This is my beloved Son, with whom I am well pleased* (Matthew 3:17). And the **Spirit of God** descended upon him in the form of a dove.

Following his baptism, Jesus went to live in the desert for forty days.

★ The beheading of John the Baptist

The death of John the Baptist

John had been given a mission: to speak out. He was not afraid to **speak the truth**. He must have been quite a character! One day, when some Pharisees had come to listen to him speak, perhaps even to spy on him, he called them a brood of vipers! That didn't please the Pharisees.

He didn't hesitate either to condemn the love affair between Herod Antipas (the son of Herod the Great) and his sister-in-law Herodias (the wife of his brother Philip). And for that, John was imprisoned. During a banquet, Salome, the daughter of Herodias, danced for Herod. He was so delighted, he promised her anything she asked. At her mother's command, Salome asked for the head of John the Baptist on a platter. And so John was beheaded.

6 JESUS' EVERYDAY LIFE

At the time of his baptism, Jesus was about thirty years old. Until then, he had been working at his carpenter's trade in Nazareth. But his baptism marked the beginning of his public ministry. He traveled throughout Galilee, Judea, and the surrounding areas announcing the Kingdom of God.

Jesus the traveler

Jesus' public ministry was very short. It lasted for only three years, during which time he traveled primarily throughout Galilee, but he also went to Judea, Samaria, Perea, the Decapolis, and all the way to Tyre and Sidon.

At the time, there was a system of **roads paved** in black stone that dated back to the time of Solomon. They were called the **royal routes** or the **king's roads**. Four principal routes went from Jerusalem: to Jericho and Perea in the east, to Samaria and Galilee in the north, toward Hebron and Egypt in the south, and toward the port of Joppa and the Mediterranean to the west. Jesus would certainly have traveled these roads. A **Roman road**, long and straight to be the shortest route possible, ran from the north to the south of Israel, passing through Samaria.

Jesus traveled from village to village on foot, like most travelers in those days, transporting any baggage on the back of a donkey. Horses were reserved for the army, and camels for crossing the desert. Jesus wore leather sandals on his feet, carried a walking stick, and used a belt to secure the folds of his tunic.

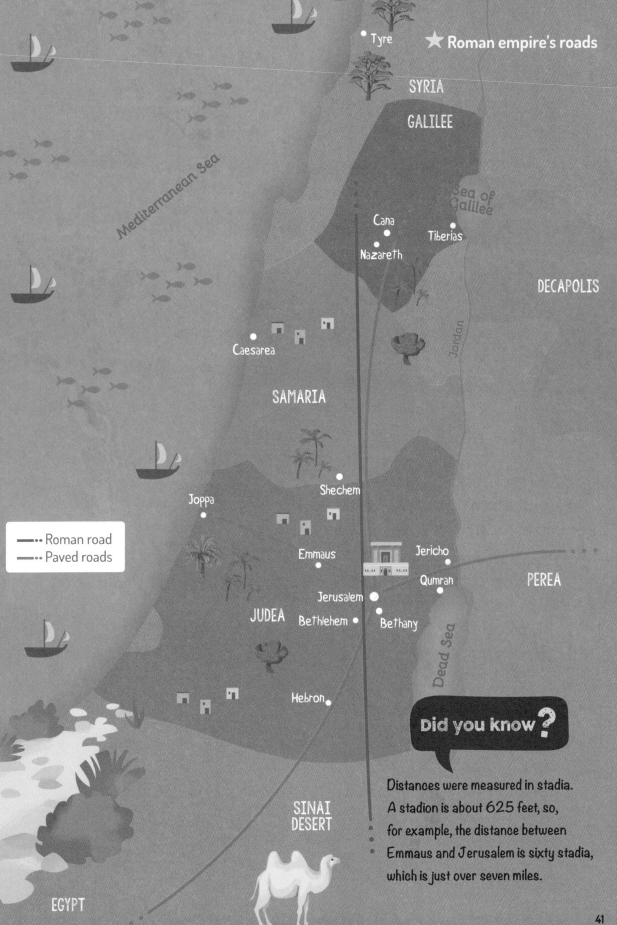

Tyre

★ **Roman empire's roads**

SYRIA

GALILEE

Sea of Galilee

Cana

Nazareth

Tiberias

DECAPOLIS

Mediterranean Sea

Caesarea

Jordan

SAMARIA

Shechem

Joppa

--•• Roman road
--•• Paved roads

Emmaus

Jericho

Qumran

PEREA

Jerusalem

JUDEA

Bethlehem

Bethany

Dead Sea

Hebron

Did you know?

Distances were measured in stadia.
A stadion is about 625 feet, so,
for example, the distance between
Emmaus and Jerusalem is sixty stadia,
which is just over seven miles.

SINAI
DESERT

EGYPT

No one is a prophet in his own land

Jesus began by visiting the cities and villages of Galilee, where he performed many healings and other miracles. Yet, when he returned to Nazareth to speak in the synagogue there, he was badly received. The people even tried to throw him off a cliff! It was then that Jesus pronounced these words which have become a well-known saying: "No one is a prophet in his own land."

Each year, Jesus would go to Jerusalem with his Apostles for the feast of Passover. They met great opposition there, above all from the Pharisees.

In the last year of his life, Jesus traveled to regions further afield. He went to Tyre and Sidon, north of Galilee; he traveled through the Decapolis, east of the Sea of Galilee; and he spent some time in Perea, across the Jordan.

Did you know?

The Jews of the time called foreigners and pagans "dogs" and referred to themselves as "the children." That's why Jesus said to the Canaanite woman, *It is not fair to take the children's bread and throw it to the dogs.* And she humorously replied, *Yes, Lord, yet even the dogs eat the crumbs that fall from their masters' table* (Matthew 15:26-27). In this way she expressed her faith that Jesus had the power to give her a small share of God's blessings on Israel.

WHERE DID JESUS LIVE?

After leaving Nazareth, Jesus no longer had a home. He said, *The Son of man has nowhere to lay his head* (Matthew 8:20). He traveled from town to town. But he often returned to Capernaum, where he perhaps had lodgings with his Apostles.

Crowds followed him

Huge crowds followed Jesus. In the episode of the multiplication of the loaves, the Gospels speak of a crowd of **5,000 men**, not counting the women and children, which would make a total of at least 10,000 people, perhaps even 30,000!

Crowds flocked from far and wide to see Jesus, to listen to him, or to be healed. Some traveled over sixty miles on foot! They came from Judea, from Jerusalem, Edom, and Perea, and from Tyre and Sidon on the coast.

One day, near Capernaum, the crowd was so big that Jesus had to get into a boat in order to be seen and heard by everyone without getting crushed. After he healed a leper, Jesus' popularity became so great that he could no longer enter a city publicly. He often withdrew to the desert to be alone and pray.

Jesus and foreigners

The Jews of the time avoided contact with foreigners; they believed they would make them impure. A Jew could not speak to or touch a pagan. Jesus called this custom into question. He was not afraid to speak to foreigners or to touch them. For example, he went to the Decapolis, inhabited by pagans, and to Samaria. And, if you recall, the Jews of the time avoided all contact with Samaritans (see page 17).

Jesus' meals

Jesus was often invited to meals, both by rich, influential people and by the poor. **Hospitality** was an important custom for the Jews, as it was all across the Middle East. A traveler was always welcomed. He wouldn't sleep in a hotel. He would present himself with the traditional greeting of peace: *Shalom*. His host would **wash his feet**, made dusty from the journey. To do him honor, he might also pour some perfume or scented oil on his feet or head. The host would listen to his guest, and call him "Master." That was what Jesus was often called. The front door would be left open so neighbors could come in and join the meal, which was often eaten outside in the courtyard or on the terrace.

The main meal was eaten at noon. One would most often eat seated on the ground or, in the Greco-Roman style, reclining on couches and leaning on the left elbow. There were no knives or forks. People **ate with their fingers**, dipping their bread in a shared sauce dish.

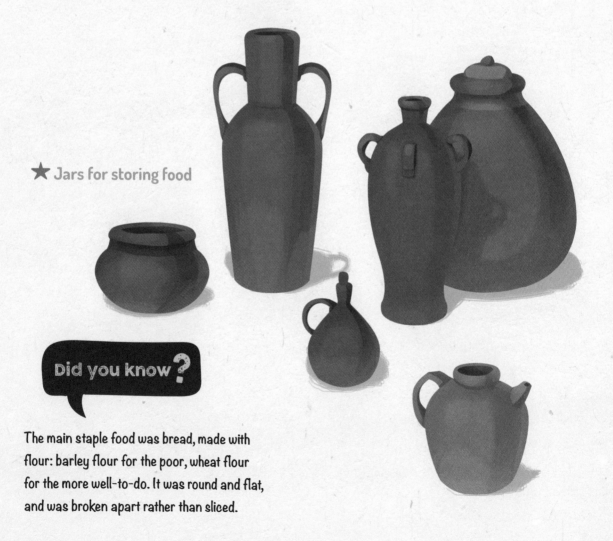

★ Jars for storing food

Did you know?

The main staple food was bread, made with flour: barley flour for the poor, wheat flour for the more well-to-do. It was round and flat, and was broken apart rather than sliced.

★ Mary grinds grain with a mortar and pestle. The meal cooks on her stove.

In Mary's kitchen

As in all rural houses, Mary's kitchen was in the courtyard, in order to let the smoke from the cooking escape. There would have been a special oven for baking bread or cakes over hot coals. Mary would grind the grain using a stone mortar and pestle. Water was kept in terracotta jars. In other jars, Mary would keep her stocks of flour, oil, and wine.

She would have had jugs, bowls, goblets, and cups. Her dishes were mainly made of terracotta or wood, although certain plates were of metal. For some better-off families, there would also be glass utensils. Since terracotta is absorbent, dishes had to be washed very carefully after each meal.

What did Jesus eat?

Bread was the staple of their diet. It was eaten at every meal. Grain (barley and wheat) was also used in many dishes and cakes.

Meat was reserved for feast days, the sabbath, and important occasions (a wedding, for instance). Each family would then kill a lamb, or sometimes an ox, a sheep, or a goat.

The Law categorized animals as pure or impure. It was forbidden to eat impure animals, including pigs and shellfish. Animals had to be slaughtered according to precise rules. Their throats had to be cut and the carcass bled, for it was forbidden to consume the blood. Game animals could be eaten, on condition that they be ritually slaughtered, as could chicken.

Fish came from the Sea of Galilee.

The most common **vegetables** were beans and lentils, onions, squash, and leeks. In the countryside, each family had its own little vegetable garden. There were many kinds of fruit that could be dried and kept in reserve for the winter, including grapes, pomegranates, figs, and dates.

There was an abundance of **butter**, **milk**, and **honey,** which were part of every child's diet.

And what did people drink? Mainly water, but also **goat's milk** and **wine**, and sometimes beer. Wine was often watered down or flavored with spices. Workers in the fields would slake their thirst with vinegar mixed with water.

Dates

Chicken

Cow

Figs

Sheep

Lentils

Squash

Beans

Onions

Barley

Pomegranate

Leeks

Grapes

Wheat

Jesus and daily rituals

Rituals were part of every meal. Hands had to be washed in a special way before each meal. The Pharisees were very insistent about this. The Essenes even required taking a ritual bath before the midday meal to purify oneself. (Have a look at pages 50–51 to see who the Pharisees and the Essenes were.)

One day, Jesus was invited to dine at the home of a Pharisee. His host was shocked that Jesus hadn't bathed beforehand. Jesus pointed out that his host had purified his body, but his heart was not pure.

★ A traditional meal

★ Traditional women's clothing

Clothing

In the time of Jesus, men did not wear pants. Instead they wore a **linen tunic** that came down to the knees.

Women wore a longer, more ample tunic so that they could carry things (like grain, for example) in its folds.

Under their tunic, men wrapped a loincloth around their waists. That was their underwear, and sometimes even their money belt!

Over the tunic, they wore a large **cloak** (*tallit*), held in place by a belt, with blue or white tassels (*tzitzit*) on the four corners. According to Mosaic Law, the tassels were to remind them of the Lord's commandments. Pharisees wore very long tassels. The cloak could be either blue or white with brown stripes. Red was reserved for military cloaks.

At the time, it was common to wear leather **sandals** secured with leather straps. Slaves walked barefoot.

Men and women covered their heads with a **veil** or a white turban, as much to protect them from the sun as for any religious reason.

Tallit

Tzitzit

★ Traditional men's clothing

Hygiene

In a hot country like Israel, it's easy to understand the need to wash hands, face, and feet often to get rid of sweat and dust. But for the Jews, hygiene was also an obligation required by the Law. More than a question of cleanliness, it was a question of **ritual purification**. The Law prescribed many acts of purification. For example, it was required to wash hands and feet upon rising in the morning, before each meal, and before going to bed.

On Friday afternoons, in preparation for the sabbath, everyone washed their entire body, either in a river or in a **ritual pool**, like those of Siloam or Bethesda in Jerusalem.

There were no bathrooms in ordinary houses. Only the wealthiest in Jerusalem could afford their own ritual baths.

People used **soap** made from plants and lye to wash both their bodies and their clothes.

After bathing, people used body oils. Women (and men too) used a great deal of **perfume**—for their clothing, their bodies, their hair, and even for their houses. Women also used makeup, especially a kind of mascara to darken the eyebrows and eyelashes.

Men wore long hair and untrimmed, oiled beards. Baldness was frowned upon. Men and women both favored curly hair. Women often braided their hair. A married woman had to veil her head in public. There were no glass mirrors; people used plates of polished metal to look at themselves, but these offered only a dim reflection.

★ **The pool of Siloam**

DIFFERENT JEWISH FACTIONS

During the Roman occupation, Jewish society went through great turmoil. Different factions developed, some favorable to the Romans, others fiercely opposed. Many were awaiting a military leader who would free them from the Romans. Jesus was to mix with all of these different groups.

Pharisees

The Pharisees sought a return to the **purity of the Law.** They refused any collaboration with King Herod and the Romans. They established a list of 613 commandments (248 positive and 365 prohibitive), which they carefully followed. They liked to debate about the Law, particularly against the Sadducees, and sometimes against Jesus. They held great sway in the synagogues and had much influence over the people. Jesus often met with Pharisees, but he had very harsh words for those who strictly followed the Law but had no compassion for sinners.

Sadducees

These were found among the aristocracy and the high priests of the Temple. They collaborated with Herod and the Romans, preferring to compromise with those in power rather than make trouble by standing up for their people. They were attached to their **wealth and power**. Despite their roles as priests, many weren't very religious. As a group, they didn't believe in the resurrection of the dead. Neither did they believe in the coming of the Messiah. It was they who decided to have Jesus put to death. They died out in A.D. 70, when the Romans destroyed the Temple.

Essenes

Very religious, the Essenes sought to be even more pure than the Pharisees, whom they saw as corrupt. They formed a sect that settled in Qumran, on the shores of the Dead Sea. They held their goods in common, had their own religious calendar, and their own rules of ritual purity. They thought that the end of the world was near and were preparing for it.

Zealots

With religious priorities more like those of the Pharisees, the Zealots were **fanatical patriots** who engaged in the political fight against the Romans. They refused to pay taxes and organized armed revolts. They saw the awaited Messiah as a real military leader. One of the Apostles, Simon the Zealot, belonged to this group before following Jesus.

SCRIBES

Even though their trade was writing, scribes were much more than public letter-writers. They were at the same time public notaries (drawing up bills of sale, marriage contracts, etc.) and attorneys. Above all, they were specialists in the sacred texts and very learned about the Law. They were called "doctors of the Law." They ensured respect for the Jewish Law and were responsible for communicating it. They were close to the Pharisees.

What's in a name?

In the Gospel, Jesus sometimes calls the Pharisees "hypocrites" for obeying the externals of the Law but not really loving God and neighbor. He also called them "white sepulchers" because they were like the tombs that were whitewashed every year: they looked beautiful on the outside but were dead on the inside.

7 THE DISCIPLES

Jesus chose twelve men, the Apostles, to help him in his mission: Simon (Peter), Andrew, James, John, Philip, Bartholomew, Thomas, Matthew, James the son of Alphaeus, Thaddeus (Jude), Simon the Zealot, and Judas Iscariot.

The call of the first disciples

The first disciples Jesus called were **fishermen** on the Sea of Galilee. Jesus was walking along the lakeshore when he spotted two brothers, **Simon** (later called **Peter**) and **Andrew**, sitting in their boat fishing. He called them. They immediately left their boat and their nets and followed Jesus.

Further along, Jesus called the brothers **James** and **John**, the sons of Zebedee. They too dropped everything and followed him. They had no doubt already heard about Jesus, for they were close to John the Baptist, who had pointed Jesus out as the Messiah.

It was no coincidence that Jesus called fishermen. For the Jews, the fish was a symbol of fruitfulness and abundance. Jesus presented himself as one who gives in abundance.

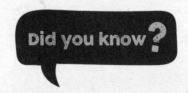

did you know?

"Apostle" comes from the Greek word *apostolos*, which means "those who are sent out." This was the term used most often by the first Christians.

4 + 8 = 12

After the fishermen Simon, Andrew, James, and John, Jesus met **Philip**, a friend of Simon and Andrew from their hometown, Bethsaida. Then he called **Bartholomew**, a friend of Philip.

Then he called **Thomas**, nicknamed Didymus, which means "twin" in Aramaic, because he had a twin brother.

In Capernaum, Jesus called **Matthew** the publican (who would later write the Gospel by that name), also called Levi. He worked at the customs post and collected taxes for the Romans. As soon as he met Jesus' gaze, Matthew got up and followed him.

The other Apostles were **James**, the son of Alphaeus, **Thaddeus**, also called Jude, **Simon the Zealot** and **Judas Iscariot**, the one who would betray Jesus.

What's in a name?

Jesus gave Simon the name *Cephas*, which means "rock" in Aramaic, because he would be the rock upon which Jesus would build his Church. And, indeed, Saint Peter became the first pope.

Jesus nicknamed James and John *Boanerges*, meaning "sons of thunder": they must have been really strong characters!

PUBLICANS AND TAX COLLECTORS

Lowly clerks responsible for collecting taxes for the Romans, publicans were detested by the people. It wasn't just that they worked for the Romans but, even worse, they often charged extra and kept that money for themselves! Unlike taxmen in high office, publicans were in direct contact with the public. That's where the name "publican" comes from. They were often considered thieves and sinners. So Jesus chose very different kinds of people to be his Apostles.

The Sea of Galilee

The Sea of Galilee (or Lake Tiberias) is a land-locked body of water in the northeast of Israel. This lake was the source of the country's freshwater supply. It was bordered by little fishing villages, like Bethsaida (whose name means "house of the fishery"), Magdala, Tiberias, and Capernaum.

The Jews were not a seafaring people. They weren't really oriented to the Mediterranean Sea. And so it was this lake that supplied most of the country's fish consumption. They fished from the schools of **small freshwater fish**, including some that are similar to sardines, carp, tilapia, and one species with spiny dorsal fins called St. Peter's fish. Twenty-two species of fish lived in the lake. Fish without fins and scales were considered unclean by the Jews, so they didn't eat catfish even though they too were to be found in the lake.

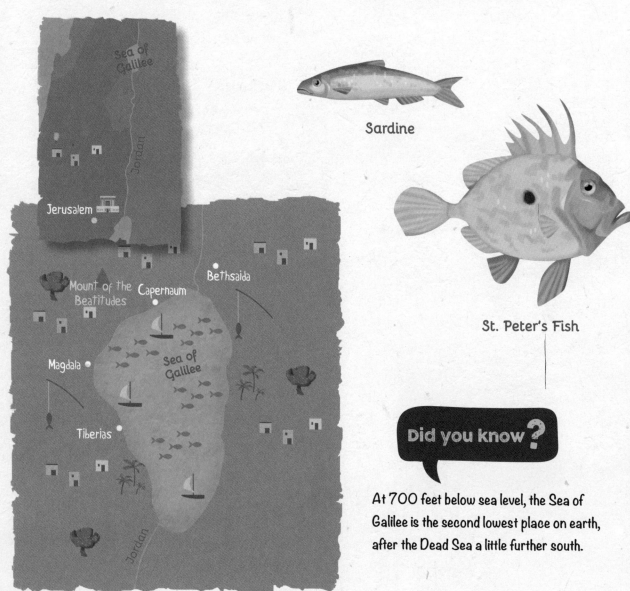

Sardine

St. Peter's Fish

Did you know?

At 700 feet below sea level, the Sea of Galilee is the second lowest place on earth, after the Dead Sea a little further south.

The fisherman's trade

In the Jewish world of the 1st century, fishermen enjoyed a good reputation. A fishing captain ran a little company of four to six men crewing two boats. They often worked as a family, like the brothers Simon and Andrew, or James and John and their father, Zebedee.

It was hard work. Fishermen often fished at night. In the Gospel, we hear Simon Peter say to Jesus, *We have fished all night and have caught nothing!*

There were several ways to fish. The simplest was **angling** from the lakeshore using a hook and line. Many hooks of the period have been found in the lakeside villages.

In shallow waters, a fisherman would stand in water up to his waist or in a boat close to the bank and use a **casting net**: he would cast (throw) a circular net weighted with stones or lead to sink it to the bottom. He would then pull it back up by a cord attached to the middle of the net.

Fishing in deep waters required a larger net, called a **seine** or **dragnet**, which could be up to 1,600 feet long. It took two boats to maneuver it into a semicircle in which the fish would be caught.

Boats in the time of Jesus were flat-bottomed and about 15 to 30 feet long. They could hold ten to twelve people. So Jesus would have been able to set out to sea with his twelve Apostles in one of these boats.

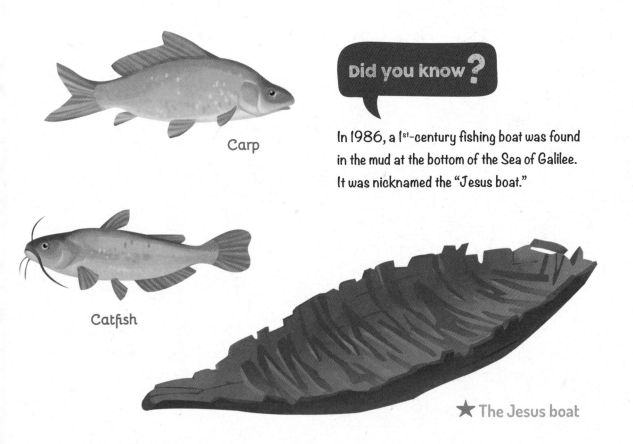

Carp

Catfish

Did you know?

In 1986, a 1st-century fishing boat was found in the mud at the bottom of the Sea of Galilee. It was nicknamed the "Jesus boat."

★ The Jesus boat

The women who followed Jesus

In addition to the twelve Apostles, many other disciples followed Jesus, both men and women. The Gospel cites several women who followed him after having been healed or freed from evil spirits: **Mary Magdalene**, **Joanna** (the wife of Herod's steward), **Mary** (the mother of James, and hence the wife of Alphaeus), **Susanna**, **Salome**, and many others who listened to his teaching and helped him financially and materially. Some women were present at the foot of the cross at the moment of his death.

This female presence close to Jesus is surprising in a society where men and women lived very separate lives outside the home. In public, a man would not speak to a woman or greet her. Jesus, however, talked with women in public and let them approach him, even women who were not Jews. Among his closest friends were two sisters, **Martha and Mary**, who often invited him to their home in Bethany, near Jerusalem.

A Jewish woman

A Jewish woman was honored and respected, especially if she was a **wife** and **mother**. The Law of Moses commanded respect for one's mother and father, recognizing the equal dignity of both.

A Jewish woman had more rights and freedom than a Roman woman of the time. However, from a legal point of view, a woman remained the responsibility of her father and, after marriage, of her husband. She could not give evidence in court and must not speak to strangers in the street. She had fewer rights than a man in public life.

In the home, on the other hand, the woman reigned supreme. She ran the house and managed the servants, if she had any. Women were in charge of spinning and weaving wool or linen to make clothing, blankets, and sheets and towels. She could even make money by selling her handiwork.

A father could promise his daughter in marriage before she reached the age of twelve. But after age twelve, she could not be wed without her consent.

The Law of Moses allowed **divorce** in serious cases (infidelity, sterility, or abuse). A man who repudiated his wife had to grant her a bill of divorce and pay the compensation specified in the marriage contract. So a woman was relatively protected.

For Jesus, though, Jewish divorce law was not enough. When the Pharisees questioned him about this, he replied that Moses had permitted divorce because men were hard-hearted. God, however, never intended for married people to divorce.

The Law was severe toward a woman who cheated on her husband. She was condemned to stoning. Stones would be thrown at her until she was dead. One day, Jesus saved a woman from such a death, saying, *Let him who is without sin among you be the first to throw a stone at her* (John 8:7). He then told her not to sin anymore.

8 THE PARABLES

Jesus liked to speak in parables. These vivid stories, drawn from agriculture and everyday life, are images of the Kingdom of God.

Agriculture at the center of life

In the time of Jesus, a large part of the population earned a living from agriculture. They grew wheat and barley, grapes and olives, and also figs, dates, and almonds. In the countryside, each family had their own vegetable garden to grow melons, onions, cucumbers, and beans. They had a few grapevines and kept goats or sheep. Jesus spoke to country people about things they knew: working in the fields and the vineyards, caring for farm animals (especially sheep and lambs), and doing work around the house.

The rhythm of the seasons

Israel has a hot climate. In Galilee, the land is fertile. But in Judea, it is arid and rocky. The year was marked by the four seasons: **spring** was from March to May, when barley and then wheat was harvested. The fields would be covered in red flowers, like the lilies of the field that Jesus spoke about, which resemble the poppy. From June to September, the **summer** was a time of heat waves. From mid-September until November came the **fall**; this was the sowing season. **Winter** lasted from December to March. In this land, trees such as olive, cypress, terebinth, and pomegranate keep their leaves in winter. Only the fig tree sheds its leaves. When its leaves sprouted again, it marked the return of spring.

The year was punctuated by **two rainy seasons**: the rains of the first season fell in the autumn, at the time of sowing; the second rains fell in the spring, causing the fields to flower again.

The Jewish calendars

The Jews had **two calendars**. The calendar of the civil year began in the month of *Tishrei*, and that of the religious year began in the month of *Nisan*.

Months were based on **lunar cycles** and lasted twenty-nine or thirty days (the time it takes for the moon to orbit the earth). A new month began as soon as one could see the new moon in the rays of the setting sun. At that moment, the Sanhedrin would declare that a new month had begun. If that didn't happen on the twenty-ninth day, the month would last for thirty days.

Since months didn't always last the same number of days, the start of the religious year was set by the Sanhedrin according to the weather and the harvest. The barley grains had to be ripe. If they weren't, an extra month called *Adar II* was added after *Adar I*. Then the year would have thirteen months and last about 384 days.

The religious calendar

The Jewish months	Time of year
Nisan	March/April
Iyar	April/May
Sivan	May/June
Tammuz	June/July
Av	July/August
Elul	August/September
Tishrei	September/October
Cheshvan	October/November
Kislev	November/December
Tevet	December/January
Shevat	January/February
Adar	February/March

★ The lunar cycle

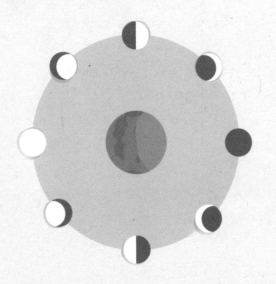

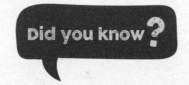
Did you know?

For Jews, the day begins at sunset. Hours are counted starting from about 6:00 PM until the morning.
The first hour of the night = 7:00 PM.
The first hour of the day = 7:00 AM.
The sixth hour of the day = 12:00 PM.
The ninth hour of the day = 3:00 PM.

★ The feast of Booths

Religious feasts

Three great religious holidays are linked to agriculture: Passover, Pentecost, and the feast of Booths.

Passover (*Pesach* in Hebrew) always falls on the fifteenth day of *Nisan* and coincides with the start of the harvest, when the barley is ripe. It lasts seven days.

Pentecost, meaning "fifty" in Greek, (or *Shavuot* in Hebrew, which means "weeks") marks the end of the harvest. It is celebrated fifty days after the start of Passover, that is,

seven weeks. It's also called the feast of the first fruits, because people would offer God the first fruits from their harvest.

The feast of Booths or of **Tabernacles** (*Sukkot* in Hebrew) takes place between September and October. It celebrates the end of the harvest and lasts seven days. Everyone would give thanks to God for the gifts of nature received during the year.

The grapevine and the olive tree

Every garden in Galilee had a **grapevine**. Grapes were also grown in vineyards surrounded by fig trees and olive trees.

As Jesus described it in one parable, the vineyard was surrounded by hedges, walls, or a fence. On the inside stood a hut or a tower from which the vinegrower could observe his vines. When the grapes were ripe, they would be thrown in a **wine press** made from a **stone vat**. The **pickers** would stand in the vat and crush the grapes with their feet.

After the grape harvest came the **harvest of olives**, which were crushed in an **olive press**. This was made of two big millstones that were turned by men or donkeys. Olive oil was used for cooking, to perfume the hair or the body, as fuel for lamps, and as medicine.

The parable of the Good Samaritan tells us that every traveler would carry wine and olive oil with him. The Samaritan took care of the wounded traveler by pouring wine over his wounds to disinfect them and oil to sooth the skin and help it heal.

A man planted a vineyard, and set a hedge around it, and dug a pit for the wine press, and built a tower.

(Mark 12:1)

★ Olive tree

★ Grapevine

★ A plowman and his plow

The sower

The **sower** was someone who often figured in Jesus' parables. We can imagine the wide movement of his arm to cast the seeds of wheat or barley. **Barley** was harvested in April *(Nisan)*, beginning on the second day of Passover. The **wheat** ripened a little later, in May. Its harvest marked the start of the feast of Booths.

Harvesting was done with a **sickle**. The sheaves were then **threshed**, or crushed underfoot by an ox, in an area in the middle of the field. Then the wheat was **winnowed**, that is, it was thrown in the air using a **pitchfork**. The breeze would blow away the straw, while the heavier grains would fall to the ground.

To prepare his field for a new crop, the plowman used a **plow** drawn either by mules or by oxen, but it was forbidden to yoke two different kinds of animals together. The plow, without wheels, was made of wood and was fitted with an iron plowshare to turn the soil.

Shepherds

Throughout the Bible, the figure of the shepherd plays an important role. Jesus said of himself, *I am the good shepherd.*

The flocks of sheep were led out to pasture shortly before Passover, in March or April. They would spend the whole summer in the fields and be brought back in before the winter, in October or November. In the evening, when the sheep went into the sheepfold for the night, a shepherd would stand at the gate and count them to be sure none were missing.

Shepherds were armed with a staff to protect themselves from wolves, who still roamed Israel in the time of Jesus.

Animals in the Gospels

Besides sheep and lambs, the animal most frequently mentioned in the Bible is the **donkey**. It was used as a beast of burden, to ride on, to draw a plow, or in a mill (to turn the millstone). Jesus rode a little donkey at his triumphal entry into Jerusalem on Palm Sunday. The horse, on the other hand, was rare and costly. It was reserved for the military.

The **camel** was commonly used in the caravans that crossed the desert.

As for **dogs**, they were looked down on in Israel. They were not kept as pets; rather, they were wild, dirty creatures that people would shoo away with their walking sticks. To the Jews, the word "dog" was an insulting term for a pagan.

But the animal most scorned by the Jews was the **pig**. They did not eat pork; it was considered unclean. In one parable, Jesus tells the story of a young man who, after spending his whole inheritance, finds himself forced to tend pigs. For a Jew, that was the worst kind of humiliation.

THE SALT OF THE EARTH

You are the salt of the earth. This well-known saying of Jesus alludes to a particular way of salting food: with salt stones. In Israel, salt came from the Dead Sea. While water normally has a 2-4% salt content, the water of the Dead Sea is about 27% salt. Stones placed in it would become coated in salt and were sold in the marketplaces. For cooking, one would simply put a salt stone in a cooking pot, and a little of its salt would dissolve into the water. But, after a little while, the stone would lose all its salt and all its zest. It then had to be replaced by a new stone. Jesus advised his disciples not to lose their zest, like those old salt stones!

★ Salt stones from the Dead Sea

The mustard seed

Jesus compared the Kingdom of God to a mustard seed. It is the tiniest of all garden seeds, but, once planted, it grows into a plant with yellow flowers that can reach almost 10 feet high. Birds like to perch in its branches and eat its seeds. Jesus must have often contemplated the sight.

Coins

In his parables, Jesus also speaks about money. At the time, Jewish, Greek, and Roman money were all in circulation in Israel.

The Roman **denarius** was a silver coin. It was engraved with the portrait of the emperor. One denarius equalled one day's wages, as we see from the parable of the laborers in the vineyard (Matthew 20:9). One laborer, having arrived at four o'clock in the afternoon, at the end of the workday, was paid a denarius, just as much as the laborers who worked a full day in the vineyard. Jesus didn't make a mistake in his arithmetic; this was a way of saying that God gives generously according to our hearts, not according to our merits.

Roman coins bearing the image of Emperor Tiberias

A little chart of exchange rates

Name of coin	Equivalent	Approx. value ($)
1 denarius	= 1 drachma	$50
1 didrachm	= 2 drachmas	$100
1 stater	= 4 drachmas	$200
1 mina	= 50 shekels	$10,000
1 silver talent	= 60 minas	$600,000

A Greek obol, or pruta

A shekel from Tyre

An ancient Greek drachma

The **drachma** was a Greek coin of the same value as the Roman denarius. The tax the Jews had to pay to the Temple each year was two drachmas. The most widely used Hebrew coin was the **stater**, also called a **silver shekel**, which was worth four drachmas.

Small change included the **assarius**, the **quadrans**, the **obol**, and the **lepton**. High value coins were the **mina** and the **talent**. The talent was a considerable sum of money. It was solid gold and weighed about 75 pounds. It was worth 12,000 drachmas!

In the **parable of the talents**, Jesus compares God to a rich man who entrusts five gold talents to one of his servants, two to another, and one to a third, and asks them to make the money grow. That was a considerable amount of money, and shows that God gives each of us many qualities which we must develop. This parable gave us the origin of the word "talent" in the sense of quality and aptitude.

Did you know?

Only Jewish coins were accepted in the Temple of Jerusalem, for there was no human face stamped on them. This accounts for the presence there of the money changers, who exchanged Greek and Roman money for Jewish coins. One day, Jesus chased them from the Temple, where they had set up their stalls without the right to do so.

A Jerusalem shekel

A silver denarius

A silver denarius from the temple of Tiberius

⁹ MIRACLES

Everywhere he went, Jesus performed miracles and healings. A miracle is an extraordinary event accomplished by the power of God. On seeing these signs, many came to believe in God.

A Jewish wedding

A Jewish marriage was the occasion of great celebrations that lasted seven days. The wedding always began on the fourth day of the week, which was **Wednesday evening**, at sunset. The bride was perfumed and adorned with jewels. A crown was placed on her head. Family and friends would lead her in a procession to the home of her future husband to the sound of singing and dancing. Once there, the couple would be seated under a canopy and receive the **blessing** of their fathers or of a local dignitary. Then came the wedding banquet. An **ox** or a **fatted calf** would be slaughtered for the occasion and served with **good wine**. The meal was led by an emcee called the master of the wedding banquet.

Upon arrival, each guest received a **wedding outfit**. That's why, in one parable, the head of the house threw out a guest who wasn't wearing a wedding garment. That showed a lack of respect for the newlyweds.

Jesus performed his first miracle at a wedding, at Cana, in Galilee. The wedding

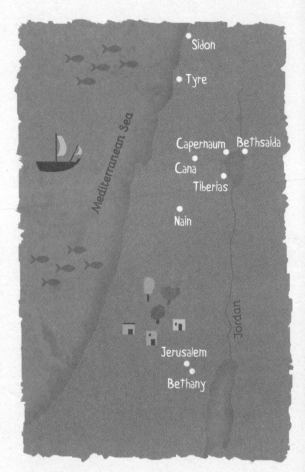

★ Sites where Jesus performed miracles

A Jewish marriage took place in three stages. First, the future spouses made a promise to each other, which they could break off at any time. Then would come the betrothal, when the man would offer his fiancée a golden ring. The couple was then considered married, but they didn't yet live together. At the end of one year, the wedding itself could be celebrated. The minimum age for marriage was eighteen for men and twelve for women.

was about to be spoiled because the wine had run out. So, at Mary's suggestion, Jesus turned water into wine. To do so, he asked the servants to fill with water the six large jugs (or jars) used for the Jewish purification rituals. Each jar could hold twenty to twenty-five gallons. That was an enormous amount of wine! And the Gospel specifies that it was excellent wine!

6 water jars

2 fish

5,000 men

5 loaves of bread

12 baskets

The multiplication of the loaves

Another time, Jesus multiplied loaves of bread and fish. It was like a giant picnic on the grassy hillsides of Galilee. Jesus fed more than 5,000 men, not counting women and children, although he had only five loaves of barley bread and two fish given by a child. The Apostles had calculated it would cost them 200 denarii to buy enough bread for such a big crowd of people. But Jesus blessed the five loaves and two fish and asked the Apostles to distribute them. The baskets never emptied! There were even twelve baskets of leftovers after everyone had eaten. In this miracle, the numbers are important symbols.

NUMERIC SYMBOLS IN THE BIBLE

5 loaves: the number 5 relates to something holy, consecrated by God.

2 fish: the number 2 is the number of division. Jesus comes to reestablish unity.

5 loaves and 2 fish (5 x 2) is a reference to the Passover meal whose number is 10 because it is linked to the tenth plague in Egypt (the death of the firstborn).

5,000 men: multiples of 5 designate those who are consecrated to God. It is an image of the Church.

12 baskets: 12 is the number of something that has been achieved, completed. It also recalls the twelve tribes of Israel and the twelve Apostles.

Did you know?

Jesus said to his Apostles, *Do not be afraid.*
These reassuring words appear 365 times in the
Bible. As many times as there are days in the year!

JESUS, MASTER OF THE ELEMENTS

The sea

The miracles of Jesus proved he had power over nature. One night on the Sea of Galilee, Jesus calmed a violent storm. Storms are a frequent occurrence on the lake. Strong winds that rise over Galilee to the west or the Golan Heights to the east funnel into the lake basin. Whirlwinds beat down on it so suddenly, they can stir up waves 10 feet high!

For the Apostles in their boat, the danger was real. Jesus was asleep. When his terrified friends woke him, he reached out his hand and ordered the sea and the wind to calm down. And the storm stopped immediately. The Apostles wondered, *What sort of man is this, that even winds and sea obey him?* (Matthew 8:27).

For the Jews, the sea was the place of the forces of evil. In ancient times, men rarely sailed the high seas. Instead, they canoed along the shore because the open sea scared them! By mastering the waves, Jesus demonstrated that he mastered both nature and evil.

A ghost!

One night, when the Apostles were in a boat crossing the Sea of Galilee, the wind stirred up the waves, and the sea became choppy. Jesus came to them, walking on the water, a few miles away from the shore, and the Apostles thought they were seeing a ghost! They were terrified. When Jesus got into the boat, the wind immediately stopped, and the Apostles were astounded (Mark 6:45-52).

The Apostles saw Jesus walking on the water in the "fourth watch of the night."
The night was divided into four watches:
from 6:00-9:00 PM was the evening;
from 9:00 PM-12:00 AM, the middle of the night;
from 12:00-3:00 AM, cockcrow;
and from 3:00-6:00 AM, the morning.

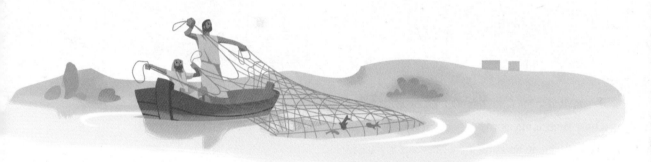

The miraculous catch of fish

The Apostles who were fishermen knew their trade well. For example, they knew that, for a good catch, it was better to fish at night. But sometimes they would fish all night and catch nothing. Jesus surprised them twice by performing miraculous catches of fish.

The first time, Peter and Andrew had fished all night without catching a thing. They were busy washing their nets, tired and gloomy. Jesus told them to go back out to sea and cast their nets into the deep. That's when the miracle happened. The net was so full of fish it was about to burst.

NUMERIC SYMBOLS

153 fish = the number of fish species known at that time. It's also the total of all the numbers from 1 to 17 (1 + 2 + 3 +... + 17 = 153). And 17 is the number that symbolizes eternal life. The number 153 means that everyone is called to eternal life.

The other miraculous catch took place after Jesus' Resurrection. Peter, James, and John, as well as few other Apostles, spent a whole night fishing without catching a thing. As they headed back to the shore, they saw a man standing on the beach. He told them to cast their net to the right, and the net filled with 153 large fish! Then they realized that the man was Jesus, risen from the dead.

SPECTACULAR HEALINGS

The man born blind

In the time of Jesus, diseases and handicaps were seen by many people as punishments sent by God. They thought that a man born blind, for example, was that way because he or his parents had sinned. Thus, many people did not take pity on the blind, who were often condemned to a life of begging in the streets.

Jesus, however, taught that illnesses and disabilities were not punishments from God but rather opportunities for the love of God to be revealed. He was moved to compassion at the sight of a sick person, and he healed many people who were suffering from incurable diseases, including leprosy and blindness. When Jesus met a man born blind in Jerusalem, he spit on the ground and, using his saliva, made some mud and applied it to the blind man's eyes. Then he told him to go wash in the **pool of Siloam** (which means "sent"). What Jesus did was common practice at the time to treat eye complaints: saliva would be mixed with some wine to make **an eyewash** that was applied to the sufferer's eyelids.

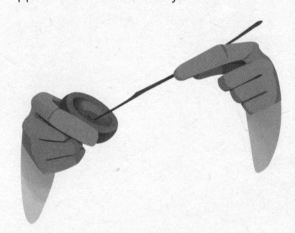

The paralytic at the pool of Bethesda

In Jerusalem, many ill people would gather at the pool of Bethesda in the hope of a cure. This pool (whose name means "house of mercy") had a special feature: it was said that, from time to time, an angel of God stirred up the water, and anyone who immersed himself in it at that moment would be cured. The ill would camp at the edge of the pool waiting for the water to bubble up. Some waited years. Jesus met a paralytic who had been waiting for thirty-eight years, and Jesus cured him in a moment!

Archeological digs have shown that this pool was fed by a natural hot spring. From time to time, the gasses that accumulated in the underground caverns would rise and stir up the water as though it were boiling.

LEPERS

Jewish society shunned lepers. To prevent the spread of this very serious disease, which produces skin sores, nerve damage, and muscle weakness, no one could touch them, and they lived far away from everyone else. Lepers had to respect strict rules prescribed by the Law of Moses. For example, they had to wear torn clothing and unkempt hair, to cover their faces down to their mouths, and to go about shouting, "Unclean! Unclean!" to make their presence known. For his part, Jesus was not afraid to approach a leper or to touch him in order to cure him.

Did you know?

Jesus always asked an ill person a question before curing him: *Do you wish to be healed?* or *What do you wish me to do for you?* He never healed by force.

★ A leper colony

The raising of Lazarus

Jesus raised Lazarus, the brother of Martha and Mary, from the dead. Lazarus had already been dead for four days when Jesus arrived in Bethany. In that hot climate, the dead were buried the same day they died. So Lazarus' body had been placed in a tomb dug out of the rock. The entrance was blocked by an **enormous round stone**.

According to the custom of the time, the corpse was placed on a ledge carved into the rock. The hands and feet were bound with **bandages** and the head covered with a cloth. The body was wrapped in a **winding sheet** and perfumed with **myrrh** and **aloe**.

Jesus asked that the stone be rolled away from the entrance to the tomb, and he called to Lazarus in a loud voice. Lazarus came out and stood there, his feet and hands still bound with bandages and his face still covered.

Did you know?

During funerals, to show one's sorrow, it was customary to weep and wail, to tear one's garments, and to roll on the ground or throw dust on one's head. Sometimes professional mourners were hired, as well as musicians who would play sad songs on the flute. On returning from a funeral, friends would offer the family of the deceased a simple "meal of condolence"—the family's first full meal since the death.

In the time of Jesus, mourning for the dead lasted for **thirty days**, during which time many things were forbidden by the Law of Moses, like shaving, wearing new clothing, or mending a torn gown. During the first three days, one could not work or respond to a greeting. The first week, one could not wear sandals, bathe, read the Law, or veil one's head. Martha and Mary would have been wearing "sackcloth and ashes": a rough gown that looked like a sack, with no sleeves or folds, with just a cord as a belt. Widows would wear this for the rest of their lives.

Jesus and the sabbath

For faithful Jews, respect for the sabbath day of rest is obligatory. Those who follow the strictest observance of the Law avoid thirty-nine different activities on that day.

In the time of Jesus some Pharisees were so strict they forbade teaching children, nursing the sick, comforting the afflicted, and almsgiving on the sabbath. Other Pharisees were more lax.

In spite of what some Pharisees thought, Jesus didn't hesitate to perform healings on the sabbath, such as when he healed the man with a withered hand in the synagogue.

THE THIRTY-NINE WORKS FORBIDDEN ON THE SABBATH

In the time of Jesus it was forbidden to do the following things on the sabbath: 1. Sow seeds, 2. Plow fields, 3. Reap crops, 4. Bind sheaves, 5. Thresh grain, 6. Winnow it, 7. Sort grain, 8. Grind it, 9. Sift it, 10. Knead dough, 11. Bake, 12. Shear wool, 13. Clean it, 14. Comb it, 15. Dye it, 16. Spin it, 17. Stretch threads, 18. Make loops, 19. Weave threads, 20. Separate threads, 21. Tie a knot, 22. Untie a knot, 23. Sew, 24. Tear cloth, 25. Trap animals, 26. Slaughter them, 27. Skin them, 28. Tan their hides, 29. Smooth them, 30. Score them for cutting, 31. Cut them into pieces, 32. Write two or more letters of the alphabet, 33. Erase something in order to write, 34. Build, 35. Tear down, 36. Extinguish a fire, 37. Light a fire, 38. Finish crafting an object, 39. Carry an object from one place to another.

Sowing seeds

Kneading dough

Weaving threads

Skinning an animal

Tying a knot

10 THE TEMPLE

The Temple in Jerusalem was the spiritual center of the Jewish people. It was God's dwelling place among them.

The Temple from Solomon to Herod

The Temple Jesus knew was the one built by Herod. It was located north of the city, on Mount Moriah.

The First Temple was built by King **Solomon** in the 10th century B.C. to house the ark of the covenant. But that Temple was destroyed by King Nebuchadnezzar when he invaded Jerusalem and took Jews as captives back to Babylon.

The Second Temple was begun in 538 B.C. under orders from the Persian king Cyrus the Great. Beginning around 20 B.C. **Herod the Great** decided to renovate and expand the Temple so that it would be as beautiful as that of Solomon. In the time of Jesus, the Temple was still under construction! But this grandiose building would not last long, for, following a Jewish uprising, it was totally demolished in A.D. 70 by **Titus**, the son of the Roman emperor Vespasian.

In the year 691, Muslims built a mosque and a shrine on the site of the Temple.

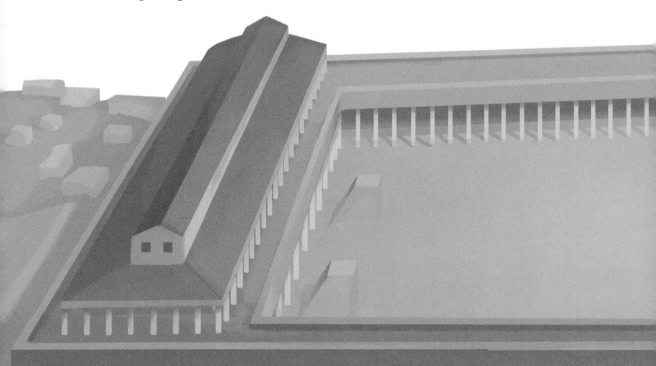

A colossal Temple

After Herod's renovation, the Second Temple was considered one of the wonders of the Mediterranean world. The exterior esplanade was twice as big as the one built by Solomon. It was over 1,500 feet long and 980 feet wide. It was supported by walls 16 feet thick built of huge stones measuring almost 40 feet long! This esplanade was called the **Court of the Gentiles** because anyone could enter it, even non-Jews. It was surrounded by **marble colonnades** where the scribes, animal sellers, and money changers could be found, and where the Pharisees and the Sadducees met to debate the Law. Jesus taught there, often contested by the scribes and the Pharisees.

★ The Temple

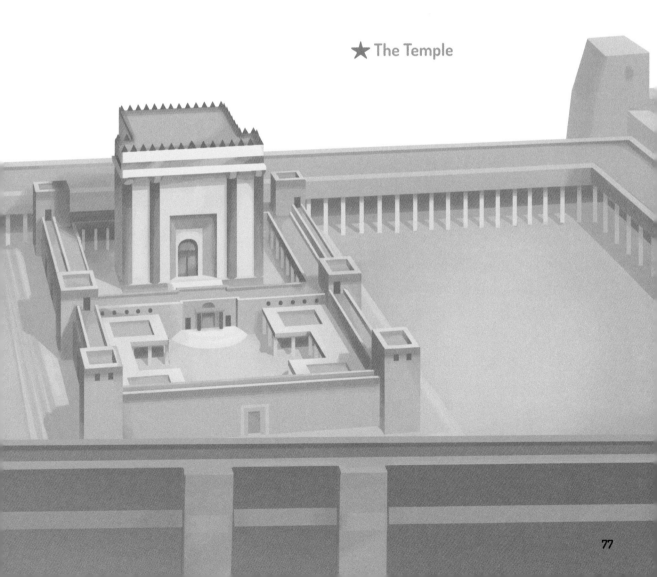

★ The Court of the Women

The interior courtyards

Beyond this esplanade were a series of other terraced courtyards reserved for the Jews. They were surrounded by a great wall. At the different entrances, stone signs warned in Greek and Latin that the area was forbidden to non-Jews on pain of death. A stone bearing this inscription was discovered in 1871.

The first courtyard was the **Court of the Women**. All Jews could enter it, unless they were impure or in mourning.

Along the walls of this courtyard was the "treasury," comprised of thirteen collection boxes for donations to the Temple. Each box was for a specific purpose indicated by a sign: for example, offerings for wood, doves, and incense; burnt offerings; and donations for the sanctuary. Jesus sometimes taught near the treasury. There he remarked on a poor widow who put two small coins into the collection box while rich people put in large sums of money. Jesus said that she gave more than all the others because she had given everything she had.

The second courtyard, five steps up from the first, was the **Court of Israel**. Only men could enter it, to take part in the animal sacrifices offered on the great high altar located a little higher up in the **Court of the Priests**. At the top of the steps of this courtyard, priests gave blessings.

The Temple merchants

For Jesus, as for all fervent Jews, the Temple was the house of God. But instead of being a house of prayer, it sometimes seemed more like a fairground.

For, indeed, in the **Court of the Gentiles**, below the royal portico, merchants and money changers would set up their stalls for business. These merchants would sell animals for sacrifice: bulls, sheep, doves, sparrows, and so on. The money changers would exchange Greek or Roman money for Hebrew coins, the only currency accepted as payment of the Temple tax of two drachmas and as donations to the treasury (see pages 66-67).

One day, in his anger, Jesus chased the money changers and the merchants from the Temple, threw over their stalls, and scattered the animals with a whip. In fact, he sent them all out where they belonged, outside the precinct of the Temple.

★ The Court of the Gentiles

The sanctuary

The sanctuary was found inside the **Court of the Priests**. It was a rectangular shaped building with walls of white stone covered inside with gold, and columns of marble and bronze. It enclosed the **Holy Place** and the **Holy of Holies**. Only priests could enter the sanctuary. They would go in through an enormous doorway made of precious metal. The roof was studded with gilded spikes to keep the birds from landing on it and soiling the building.

In the first room, the Holy Place, was the **altar of incense**, covered in gold, where incense was burned morning and evening, as well as the seven-branched candelabra (the *menorah*), and the table of showbread, on which twelves loaves of bread symbolized the twelve tribes of Israel.

A great **veil**, or curtain, separated this room from the Holy of Holies. This was the veil that was torn in two at the moment of Jesus' death on the cross. The Holy of Holies is the most sacred place in the Temple, the place of the presence of God. In Solomon's Temple, it housed the ark of the covenant. But the ark of the covenant disappeared at the time of the Babylonian exile, and the Holy of Holies had remained empty ever since. Once a year, the high priest would enter it to offer incense on the Day of Atonement (*Yom Kippur*).

To the sides of the sanctuary were rooms set aside for the storage of wood, water, lambs, bread, and a perpetual fire that was permanently lit, as well as the hall of the Sanhedrin, where the assembly of seventy elders would gather, presided over by the high priest. (To learn more about the Sanhedrin, see page 87.)

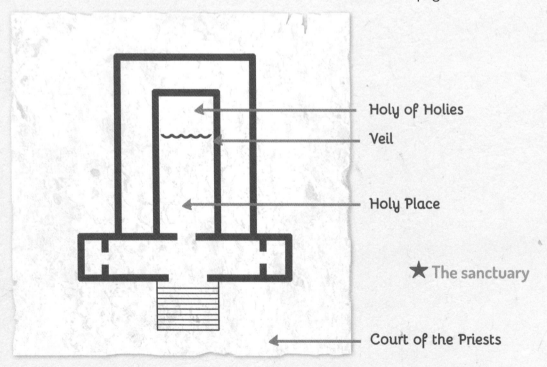

Holy of Holies

Veil

Holy Place

★ The sanctuary

Court of the Priests

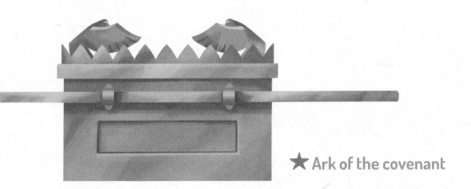

★ Ark of the covenant

The ark of the covenant

The ark of the covenant housed the tablets of the Law given by God to Moses on Mount Sinai (the Ten Commandments). It was a chest of acacia wood covered in gold and surmounted by two cherubim with curved wings. It had been carried on poles to accompany the Hebrews in their conquest of the Promised Land.

It was later placed in the Temple by King Solomon. Shortly before the fall of Jerusalem to the Babylonians, in the 6th century B.C., it is said to have been hidden in a grotto by the prophet Jeremiah to protect it from theft. Since then, no one knows what became of it. Many legends surround this ark that so mysteriously disappeared.

★ Menorah

The menorah

There was only one *menorah*, or seven-branched candelabra, in the whole kingdom, and it was housed in the Temple. Solid gold and tall as a man, it represented a tree, with one central branch and three on each side, decorated with golden almond blossoms. Its seven oil lamps burned day and night in the Temple as a symbol of the perpetual divine presence. It was stolen and carried off to Rome as booty at the time of the destruction of the Temple by the Romans in A.D. 70. Since then, all trace of it has been lost.

Priests and Levites

Priests were all descendants of **Aaron**, the brother of Moses. They were divided into twenty-four families who took turns serving in the Temple each week. The role of the priests was above all to carry out the animal sacrifices. They were called **sanctifiers**. They also sang hymns, offered up incense, and recited prayers during the ceremonies.

Priests as a whole were led by the **high priest**. He was chosen by the Romans when they governed Judea. The high priest also presided over the Sanhedrin (the Jewish assembly that made decisions concerning religious matters and acted as a tribunal).

Normally the high priest was appointed for life, but, for political reasons, there was a whole succession of high priests during the 1st century. Sometimes, they even bought their position. At the time of the death of Jesus, Caiaphas was the high priest.

The **Levites**, descendants of the tribe of **Levi** (which included Moses and Aaron), were responsible for the care of the Temple, its upkeep and security. Thus, they were priests but not sanctifiers.

The priests' vestments

Priests wore a white linen **ephod**, a sort of tunic, with an embroidered belt and, on their heads, a linen turban, or miter, secured in place with a ribbon. A second headband was wrapped around this turban. They went barefoot, for the Temple was holy ground (in the same way that Moses removed his sandals before the burning bush).

Over this outfit, the high priest also wore a robe hemmed with little golden bells and a sort of vest woven out of threads of gold and dyed linen (purple, violet, and crimson), with a gold breastplate set with twelve precious gems as a reminder of the twelve tribes of Israel.

★ High priest

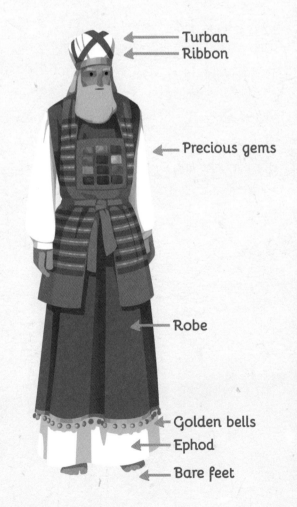

- Turban
- Ribbon
- Precious gems
- Robe
- Golden bells
- Ephod
- Bare feet

The Temple liturgy

At sunrise, priests would go up to the Temple roof and watch for the first rays of the sun. They would then sound the trumpet to awaken the inhabitants of Jerusalem.

Then, during the morning service, priests sacrificed a lamb as an offering to God on behalf of the people of Israel. The service continued with prayers (as in the synagogues) and a reading of a passage of the Law. Then a priest, chosen by lot, entered the Holy Place to burn incense on the altar of gold. The little bells at the hem of his vestment would tinkle as he walked and alert the people that the incense offering was about to commence. Levites played music while the priest remained alone in the sanctuary. Next, part of the lamb that had been sacrificed was burned on the altar, on which the priest also poured some wine. The rest of the lamb was eaten by the priests and the Levites. A trumpet blast marked the end of the morning service.

At three o'clock in the afternoon there was a short prayer of blessing.

In the evening, between sunset and nighttime, there was a second sacrifice of a lamb, accompanied by the singing of psalms and a blessing.

Throughout the whole day, anyone could offer an ox, a sheep, or pigeons in sacrifice to give thanks, for a family event, or in atonement for a sin. Doves were sacrificed for a woman's purification forty days after giving birth; little sparrows could be offered for the healing of a leper.

What's in a name?
The **shofar** is a ram's horn the Temple priests used during the morning service and for certain feasts.

11 JESUS' LAST DAYS

When Jesus went up to Jerusalem for the feast of Passover, he knew he was about to die.

The last Passover

The final week of Christ's life was spent in Jerusalem. Jesus went there with his disciples for the feast of Passover. Like him, every year on this occasion, many Jews went on pilgrimage to the Temple.

Jesus entered the city with both humility and solemnity. He was seated on a donkey, a beast of burden, which he had sent for beforehand from the village of Bethpage ("the house of figs") on the Mount of Olives. He entered Jerusalem by the Golden Gate, a monumental portal that led to the Temple

from the east. All along his route, he was hailed by a crowd waving palm branches and paving the way before him with their cloaks.

They recognized Jesus as the Messiah, whose entrance into the city had been foretold by the prophet Zechariah: *Behold, your king comes to you; humble and riding on a donkey.*

This all happened the Sunday before the Resurrection, which Christians call Palm Sunday.

THE JEWISH PASSOVER

Passover commemorates the flight of the Hebrews from Egypt in about 1445 B.C. On the night of their deliverance from slavery, God commanded his people to sacrifice a one-year-old lamb "without blemish" and to eat it with unleavened bread and bitter herbs. The Law of Moses established the annual celebration of Passover, which Jesus observed with his Apostles on the night before he died, and which faithful Jews still celebrate today.

Bethany

During the last week of his life, Jesus visited the home of his friends Martha, Mary, and Lazarus (the one whom Jesus had raised from the dead) in Bethany, about two miles from Jerusalem. Bethany means "the house of dates."

The Last Supper

On Thursday evening, Jesus ate his Last Supper with his twelve Apostles. They gathered in the upper chamber (or **cenacle**, from the Latin *cena*, meaning meal) of a house in Jerusalem. It was a covered room built on the flat roof of a house, and was reached by an outside staircase. It could be used as a guest room or a dining room.

This supper was the first meal of the feast of Passover (the Jewish *seder*). During this meal, Jews celebrate the flight of the Hebrews from Egypt. They eat flat, **unleavened bread** (without yeast) to recall the bread the Hebrews hurriedly ate just before leaving Egypt: they hadn't had time to allow the bread to rise. Jesus blessed this bread and broke it in several pieces to be shared with everyone according to Passover tradition. On the table were also the **four traditional cups of wine**, which would also be blessed and shared.

THE FIRST MASS

After Jesus blessed and broke the bread, he said to his Apostles: *Take this, all of you, and eat of it, for this is my body, which will be given up for you. Do this in memory of me.* Ever since, at each Mass, priests the world over do the same as they repeat Jesus' words, making him present in the form of bread and wine.

The arrest of Jesus

After the meal, Jesus went out with his Apostles to the **garden of Gethsemane**. But one of them was missing. Judas, who had agreed to betray Jesus for **thirty pieces of silver** (about a month's salary), had left to fetch people to arrest Jesus.

In the garden of Gethsemane, Jesus willingly laid down his life for the salvation of the world. Judas arrived in the garden with a band of men armed with swords and clubs. They had been sent by the leaders of the priests, the scribes, and the elders. As a signal to identify the man they were to arrest, Judas kissed Jesus.

Ever since, the expression "the kiss of Judas" is used to speak of an act of betrayal.

THE GARDEN OF GETHSEMANE

The garden where Jesus was arrested is at the base of the Mount of Olives, to the east of Jerusalem in the Kidron Valley. The fruit of its olive trees was used to supply the Temple with oil. A great deal of it was required for its many oil lamps. The name Gethsemane means "olive press."

The trial

Jesus was led before several people who would decide his fate. He was first taken in the middle of the night to the priest **Annas**, the father-in-law of **Caiaphas**, who was the high priest that year. Both were Sadducees from aristocratic families. They had been looking for a way to have Jesus put to death for some time already. Annas was no longer the high priest, but he still carried great authority. He questioned Jesus, and then sent him bound in chains to Caiaphas, who interrogated him before the assembled **Sanhedrin**.

This trial was in fact illegal, for it took place in the middle of the night, something forbidden by the Law. The Sanhedrin called false witnesses to testify against Jesus, because the Law stated that the testimony

Did you know?

I wash my hands of this man's blood.
Pilate had no wish to have Jesus killed, but he gave in at the insistence of the crowd. He washed his hands to signify: "I am not responsible for this death." The expression "I wash my hands of it" means that you don't feel responsible for what's happening.

THE SANHEDRIN

The Sanhedrin was the Jewish assembly that dealt with the religious and domestic affairs of the country. It served as a tribunal and could condemn people to death. In Jerusalem, it was comprised of seventy members, plus the presiding high priest. They were priests, elders from the leading Jewish families, and scribes. Its members were almost all Sadducees close to the government. Each town and city had its own small local Sanhedrin of seven members. The Jerusalem Sanhedrin convened regularly in a room set aside for them within the Temple, in the Court of the Priests. But Jesus' trial took place in Caiaphas' private home.

of two witnesses was enough to convict anyone who incited public unrest. Jesus remained silent throughout the whole trial. Finally, Caiaphas asked him if he was the son of God. Jesus replied, "I am." That was enough to convict him of blasphemy and to put him to death. According to Jewish Law, anyone who dared to say he was God was sentenced to death by stoning.

However, the Sanhedrin wanted the Romans to condemn him to death, for they feared a public uprising. So they sent Jesus to **Pilate**, the Roman governor of Judea. In the early hours of the morning, Jesus was taken to the **praetorium**. In a palace built by Herod, it was the home of Pilate and the place where he rendered justice.

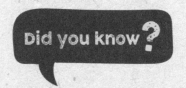
The word "Passion" comes from the Latin *passio*, which means "to suffer." It is the word used to describe Jesus' suffering, from his arrest to his death on the cross.

The Passion

Jesus' Passion began with slaps, spitting, and mockery from the high priest's guards. Then, on Pilate's order, Jesus was flogged. **Scourging** was the whipping of a criminal bound to a pillar, or column. The whip had straps with balls of lead or pieces of sheep bone on the ends (the *flagellum*). It was a particularly cruel form of punishment. Hebrew law limited the number of lashes to forty. But for the Romans there was no limit.

After the Roman soldiers flogged Jesus they dressed him in a purple robe or cloak and put a **crown of thorns** on his head. The purple robe (dyed with a shellfish extract called *purpura*) was reserved for the Roman emperor; the soldiers made Jesus wear it to mock him, calling him the "king of the Jews." They placed a reed in his hand as his royal scepter. The crown of thorns was woven from the branches of a creeping plant with long thorns that grew on the outskirts of Jerusalem and was used as kindling or to tie up bundles of wood.

The crown of thorns in Paris

The crown of thorns was for a time in the possession of Byzantine emperors before being given as guaranty to Venetian bankers, and then recovered by Saint Louis of France in 1239. It was held for 500 years in Paris' Sainte-Chapelle ("Holy Chapel"), which was specially built to house it. Since 1896, it has been kept in the treasury of Notre-Dame Cathedral, and presented to the faithful every first Friday of the month, at 3:00 PM, the time of Jesus death.

Crown of thorns

Hammer

Nails

Flagellum

Pillar

The torture of the cross

Crucifixion was a punishment practiced by the Romans from about 200 B.C. It was reserved for non-Roman citizens, bandits, pirates, murderers, and rebels.

Jesus was crucified rather than stoned because his death sentence was handed down by Pilate for rebellion against the Roman emperor. He was executed along with two thieves, one on his left and one on his right.

Crucifixions were carried out outside the city in a place called **Golgotha**, which means "place of the skull."

As Jesus was led from the praetorium to Golgotha, he carried his own cross until the soldiers forced a man passing by to carry it for him. In fact, the part of the cross carried by Jesus was the horizontal beam, called the **patibulum**, which weighed about 45–65 pounds.

Once at the place of execution, Jesus' wrists were nailed to the horizontal beam and his feet were nailed to the vertical beam. The cross was then hoisted up and fixed firmly in the ground. As the weight of his body pulled on his arms, Jesus died of suffocation.

Jesus' agony lasted for six hours. He was placed on the cross at the third hour, which is 9:00 AM, and he died at the twelfth hour, which is 3:00 PM.

At that moment, on Friday the 14th in the month of Nisan, on the eve of Passover, the Temple priests were beginning the slaughter of the Passover lambs. Jesus was the Lamb of God, who offered his life for the sins of the world.

Did you know?

Jesus didn't carry his cross all alone! The Romans forced a man on his way back from the fields, Simon of Cyrene, to help him. Cyrene was a Greek colony in modern Libya, in northern Africa, where there was a large Jewish community.

The burial

The bodies of the condemned were normally thrown in a **common grave** near the place of execution.

But that wasn't the case for Jesus. A rich disciple of his, **Joseph of Arimathea**, a member of the Sanhedrin, asked Pilate for Jesus' body and laid it to rest in a new tomb that he had built for himself.

This tomb carved out of the rock looked the same as those of all rich families. It had a small entrance and a chamber where the body was laid on a stone bench. There could be several benches for different members of the same family. The square-shaped entrance was sealed off with a heavy round stone rolled across it on a track dug into the ground.

For reasons of hygiene, **tombs** were always located outside the city. They had to be at least 50 cubits, or about 75 feet, away from the wall of the city. Wealthy families built their tombs on their own property. **Cemeteries** were rare, and were reserved for foreigners and the poor.

The preparation of the corpse

According to Jewish custom, particular care was taken of the body before it was placed in the tomb. First, the corpse's eyes were shut. Then the body was washed with water and rubbed with spices and perfumes, of which the most common were **myrrh** and **aloe**. It was wrapped in a white linen cloth called a **shroud**. The face was covered with a smaller cloth called a **sudarium**.

Since Jesus died on a Friday, on the eve of Passover, his friends didn't have time to wash and anoint his body. They simply wrapped it in a shroud, covered his face with a sudarium, and quickly laid the body in the tomb before sunset marked the beginning of the sabbath.

The sabbath ended at sundown on Saturday. At dawn on Sunday, some women went back to the tomb with spices and perfumes to finish the burial preparations.

The Shroud of Turin

A shroud is preserved in the Italian city of Turin. It bears the traces of a man's body that had been flogged and crucified. His head had been wounded by thorns, and his right side had been pierced by a lance. Could it be the burial shroud of Jesus? Many people believe that it is.

★ A traditional burial

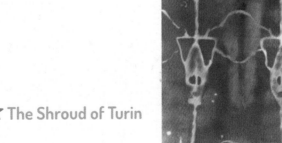

★ The Shroud of Turin

The Resurrection

Pilate stationed a guard of Roman soldiers at Jesus' tomb. Jesus had foretold that he would rise on the third day, and the Jewish leaders were afraid that Jesus' friends might come and steal his body to make people think he had been resurrected. Despite the guards and the heavy stone sealing off the entrance, the Sunday after Jesus' death, the tomb was empty!

Women were the first to proclaim the Resurrection of Jesus. When they went to the tomb early on Sunday morning to anoint his body, they found the tomb empty. Who could have rolled the stone away? It weighed more than a ton. The women would never have had the strength to do it, and had been worrying about who would do it for them. The soldiers, gripped by fear, had fled.

According to the Gospels, the women saw **angels**. In Matthew, an angel rolled the stone away and was sitting on it. In the Gospel of Mark, the women saw an angel seated inside the tomb. In Luke, there were two angels who spoke to the women. As God's messengers, angels announced the Resurrection.

In Jewish Law, a woman's word didn't carry as much weight as that of a man, yet the risen Jesus chose to appear to women first! But when they told the disciples, they couldn't believe them! Peter and John ran to the tomb to see for themselves.

The glorified body

After his Resurrection, Jesus appeared first to **Mary Magdalene**. But she didn't recognize him, and thought he was the gardener. Jesus wasn't exactly the same as before. And yet it really was him, with his body, the same facial features, the same voice—and the marks of the nails and the lance wound in his pierced side. The term Christians use to speak of the body of Jesus after the Resurrection is his **glorified body**, that is to say, his body perfected by the glory of God. Jesus promised that at the end of time he will come again; then all the dead will rise again with their bodies.

Jesus' glorified body was supernatural and natural at the same time. On one hand, he could appear and disappear, as on the evening when the Apostles were gathered together in a room behind a locked door and Jesus suddenly appeared among them.

On the other hand, Jesus retained his humanity. He showed Thomas the marks of the nails and the wound in his side. Thomas, who had refused to believe in the Resurrection unless he could see the risen Jesus, touched Jesus' wounds with his hands and believed. Jesus also ate with his Apostles after his Resurrection.

THE ASCENSION

After spending forty days with his disciples, Jesus ascended into heaven. Christians celebrate this event with the feast of the Ascension. The name comes from the Latin *ascensio*, meaning "to rise up." On the summit of the Mount of Olives, Jesus told his Apostles to spread his word throughout the world. Then he rose and vanished from their sight.

Under the direction of Romain Lizé, Vice President, Magnificat

Editor, Magnificat: Isabelle Galmiche
Editor, Ignatius: Vivian Dudro
Translator: Janet Chevrier
Proofreader: Claire Gilligan
Assistant to the Editor: Pascale van de Walle
Layout Designers: Armelle Riva, Gauthier Delauné
Production: Thierry Dubus, Sabine Marioni

Original French edition: *Qui est Jésus: Sa Vie, son Pays, son Temps*
© 2017 by Mame, Paris.
© 2018 by Magnificat, New York • Ignatius Press, San Francisco
All rights reserved.
ISBN Ignatius Press 978-1-62164-235-0 • ISBN Magnificat 978-1-941709-56-6

Printed in January 2018 by Tien Wah Press, Malaysia
Job number MGN 18004
Printed in compliance with the Consumer Protection Safety Act, 2008